AMERICAN ELF

THE COLLECTED SKETCHBOOK
DIARIES OF JAMES KOCHALKA

BOOK THREE

JANUARY 1, 2006 TO
DECEMBER 31, 2007

TOP SHELF PRODUCTIONS, MARIETTA, GA

It's extremely difficult to write this introduction.

This is like my 5th try.

The book itself isn't so complicated. It's just another volume of my diary comic strip.

Yup.

But it's also my LIFE.

All my hopes and dreams and joys and failures.

Silly & serious

And my family! My family is a huge part of this book.

This book is everything.

YOU CAN ALSO READ NEW STRIPS DAILY AT AMERICANELF.COM

by Daniel Handler + Lisa Brown

American Elf (Book 3) © & ™ 2008 James Kochalka. Published by Top Shelf Productions, PO Box 1282, Marietta GA 30061-1282, USA. Layout by Christopher Ross. Publishers: Brett Warnock and Chris Staros. Top Shelf Productions® and the Top Shelf logo are registered trademarks of Top Shelf Productions, Inc. All Rights Reserved. No part of this publication may be reproduced without permission, except for small excerpts for purposes of review. First Printing, November 2008. Printed in China.

Visit our online catalog at www.topshelfcomix.com.

ISBN 978-1-60309-016-2
1. Graphic Novels
2. Autobiography
3. Cartoons/Cartoon Art

TODAY IS THE 20th ANNIVERSARY

OF OUR FIRST KISS
(BUT I GAVE AMY ALL HER PRESENTS YESTERDAY)

I love you!

I KNOW

I've told you twenty times today.

Have you?

I guess that's why I know.

JANUARY 1, 2006

WRINKLES

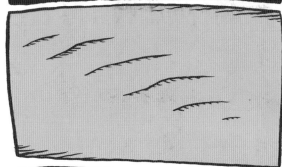

Look, the sky is wrinkled.

Pretty

JANUARY 2, 2006

PAJAMA DREAMS

Did you have any dreams last night?

No.

Where'd my dreams go?

Don't worry, I'm sure they'll come back tonight.

In my pajamas!

JANUARY 3, 2006

WESLEY

SOME GIRL WAS ON HER WAY TO BE AN INTERN AT DRAWN & QUARTERLY IN MONTREAL, BUT SHE WAS TURNED AWAY AT THE BORDER. SHE ENDED UP STAYING THE NIGHT AT OUR HOUSE.

What's that girl's name?

Wesley

Leslie?

THE NEXT MORNING

Daddy? Come.

Oh! she woke up

See!

JANUARY 4, 2006

FOOD

My hot dog smells like mildew

maybe it's not the hot dog... maybe it's your fingers.

You're right

JANUARY 4, 2006

FOOD

Look daddy

Cereal dancing

JANUARY 5, 2006

IMPORTANCE

You're tall.

I'm standing on a chair

I usually think of myself as being taller than everyone...

...but they say I'm actually quite short.

JANUARY 6, 2006

HAPPINESS

La da da

THERE'S AN OPPORTUNITY to have fun almost every second of the day.

And if nothing's going on, you can sing a little song...

OR make animal noises

Roar

JANUARY 7, 2006

ELATED

What's your problem today?

Today?

I'm like this every day!

Do you want to stay home while me and Eli play at the gym without you?

Yeah! I'll stay home and DRAW!

JANUARY 8, 2006

OBSERVED BY DEMONS

JANUARY 9, 2006
I GET THIS FEELING WHILE I SLEEP
THAT CREATURES ARE WATCHING ME.

SELF-DOUBT

I hope that pimple goes away before my rock show on thursday

How can I rock with a pimple?

How can I rock when I'm going bald?!

JANUARY 10, 2006

BEDTIME STORY

WAAAAAA DADDY

James

Eli... go back to sleep

DADDY, STORY

WAAA

Stop it!

THE NEXT MORNING

then Daddy say "Stop it!"

JANUARY 11, 2006

ROCK STAR

Hi Mom.

You want me to sing at your church's spaghetti dinner?

Amyyyyy

JANUARY 12, 2006

THE POETRY OF NIGHT SCIENCE

JANUARY 13, 2006

PIZZA MONEY

JANUARY 14, 2006

SHOVELING FOOTPRINTS

JANUARY 15, 2006

ASH DUMPER

JANUARY 16, 2006

♥ HACK

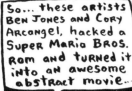

So... these artists Ben Jones and Cory Arcangel, hacked a Super Mario Bros. rom and turned it into an awesome abstract movie...

uh huh

Anyhow... I opened it up in "text edit" and it was all gobbledygook, except for a small bit of text.

...Then I changed the text so when you run their hack it says "Amy I love you"

Well! Romance is alive & well in your house.

Amy wasn't impressed at all.

well...

JANUARY 21, 2006

SUPER DIAPER WOW

That's a BIG poo poo

le' me see it

I want see big poo poo

You really want to see it?

Yes!

Oh!

JANUARY 22, 2006

TWO WINDOWS

RIGHT OUTSIDE OUR WINDOW IS THE NEIGHBOR'S WINDOW

STILL, I NEVER SEEM TO WITNESS CRIMES OVER THERE ANYMORE.

Eek!

I hate it when they look me in the eye!

JANUARY 23, 2006

THAT JAMES KOCHALKA GUY

BUYING "THE COMICS JOURNAL" AT BORDERS

Hey, are you that James Kochalka guy?

Yes I am

I sent you a copy of my book. It was a little gray book called "tommorrow we revolutionize"

uh oh

I don't remember that book—

Um...

You wrote me a very nice letter!

Oh, GOOD!! I'm glad I didn't blow you off!

JANUARY 24, 2006

SNOWBALL KISSER

KISS

ha ha ha

Eli, don't eat your snowball.

I not eating. I kiss!

KISS

hee hee hee

JANUARY 25, 2006

I MAKE MARIO RUN WHILE ELI MANS THE JUMP BUTTON

Jump! Push the button!

The mushroom man is coming! Push the button! Push the button! Push the button

PUSH THE BUTTON

Yes! We did it!

JANUARY 26, 2006

BASMATI RICE STORM

Here come our foods

Yay!

Oops   Aah!

I'm so sorry!

My rice!

Waah

LATER, WE ALL THOUGHT IT WAS PRETTY FUNNY

Would you like some more rice? Should I dump it on your head?

Ha ha

JANUARY 27, 2006

SPAGHETTI ILLUSION

AMY DRIVES US TO SPRINGFIELD, VERMONT-

The world is sure filled with a lot of stuff!

It would be a shame if it were all illusion

-WHERE MY MOM MAKES ME SING MY SONG "HOCKEY MONKEY" AT HER CHURCH'S SPAGHETTI DINNER AND CABARET.

All the scientists are running around ♪

JANUARY 28, 2006

HELLO WORLD

THE PHONE KEEPS RINGING, CALL AFTER CALL

Should I answer it?

RING

Hi, Josh!

Me and Amy are having a date!

JANUARY 29, 2006

FRANKLY BIRTHDAY

JIM WOODRING'S "VISIONS OF FRANK" DVD

More Frank!

No, honey... we have to to go to the restaurant for Mommy's special birthday dinner

AT THE RESTAURANT

BLUCK

I feel better!

I'll run to "Old Navy" and buy him some new clothes

JANUARY 30, 2006

ACROSS THE VOID

AN ERASER CRUMBLY TUMBLED DIAGONALLY ACROSS MY SKETCHBOOK,

OVER GHOSTS OF ERASED PENCIL LINES, IT ROLLED

PAST THE TIP OF MY PENCIL WHICH PAUSED IN ADMIRATION OF ITS GRACEFUL DESCENT

ACROSS THE VOID

JANUARY 31, 2006

CAT TAIL

Do you want a cat tail?

yes

At least I think they're called "cat tails"...

It looks more like a hot dog on a stick.

Do you want a hot dog for lunch?

FEBRUARY 1, 2006

EVIDENCE

BEHIND THE GARAGE

There's another drop of blood. And another!

'Some one dying?'

No... its probably an animal

We didn't do it! We are innocent!

FEBRUARY 2, 2006

THE BAG

Is it about a year since the killer dumped his clothes down the bank?

Yes

Maybe the blood we saw yesterday dripped from the GHOST of the BLOODY BAG!

Stop scaring everyone!

FEBRUARY 3, 2006

WINDING DOWN

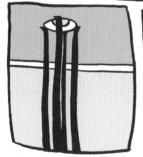

PLUCK

Don't WORRY! Just because I'm taking down the decorations doesn't mean the party's over.

AMY'S PARTY

FEBRUARY 4, 2006

31 × 30

31 × 30. I think that's my size

I can't remember

why don't you try them on

Nah

I don't have any money with me.

I'll come back later

But you could try them on NOW and...

No!

FEBRUARY 5, 2006

AUTOMATRIX

Panel 1: Can I get a receipt for my computer time & print-outs?

Panel 2: You can just put your credit card in the self-serve machine there and print a receipt.

No! I tried.

Panel 3: My card would only go half-way in

Panel 4: That's not a credit card. It's an I.D.

Oh, whoops!

funny

FEBRUARY 6, 2006

GROCERY SHOPPERS

Panel 1: Do you want to come to the grocery store with me?

Panel 2: Will you be really sexy at the store?

Yes

Panel 3: Oooh!

I do want to come too, then.

It'll be fun

FEBRUARY 7, 2006

EMOTIONAL BOOOOOOOOOOOOOOTS

Panel 1: Eli? What's wrong? Get up and get your jacket on

I sad

Panel 2: Why are you sad?

Panel 3: My boots sad!

FEBRUARY 8, 2006

ELF DAD

Panel 1: Where's your big ear?

huh?

Panel 2: You mean the big ears that I have in the drawings in my comics?

Yes

Panel 3: That's only in the drawings

Oh

FEBRUARY 9, 2006

A LITTLE HUNGOVER & RECORDING A SONG AT THE FIGHT FACTORY

Fuck! Colin, God damnit

James! You said you wouldn't fight with me this time.

well...

I guess I should've got it in writing!

I'm dizzy

FEBRUARY 10, 2006

ANOTHER TIME

How was Recording today?

Oh, we didn't do anything. Eric went to fedex while me & Jason waited for him.

But Jason said I could have his Playstation 2

except then he wouldn't let me take it.

He said I could another time...

FEBRUARY 11, 2006

DADDY STAR WARS

Daddy?

Are you Star Wars?

Yes. I am.

FEBRUARY 12, 2006

SHOTGUN

So...

Vice President Dick Chenney shot his friend in the face!

For Real?

FEBRUARY 13, 2006

THE SECRET OF LOVE

LAST NIGHT:

We'll give mommy this Valentine in the morning.

Remember, don't tell mommy. It's a secret!

Shhh

Secret!

FEBRUARY 14, 2006

DARK BOTTLE

I wonder if any wine is left in that bottle? It's sort of too dark to see in.

Oh, don't look. I don't want any right now.

Do I?

FEBRUARY 15, 2006

THE STINK OF EVIL

ELI HAS A FEVER.

I'M IN BED, PLAYING RESIDENT EVIL WITH THE COVERS PULLED OVER MY HEAD.

IN THIS ENCLOSED SPACE, I SMELL THE STINK OF MY BREATH.

SNIF SNIF

I HAD FORGOTTEN TO BRUSH MY TEETH YET.

FEBRUARY 16, 2006

HAPPY STICK

Nice Stick!

I CARRY IT HOME TO BURN IN THE FIRE.

A VERY HAPPY LOOKING DUDE IN A CAR GOING BY GIVES ME A "THUMBS UP"

Ha Ha

He really liked my Stick!

FEBRUARY 17, 2006

NERVOUS FACTS

Um... what was I calling you about?

I'm embarrassed to ask.

Well, I got the final version of my children's book contract with Random House and I noticed that all payments go to my AGENT, not to me directly.

Is that... normal? I guess that's pretty normal, right?

FEBRUARY 18, 2006

EVIL BED

I PLAYED "RESIDENT EVIL" IN BED FOR A WHILE

...BEFORE PUTTING IT DOWN AND GOING TO SLEEP.

LATER, AMY CAME UP TO BED & WE STARTED FOOLING AROUND & STUFF

Ooh
mmm

BUT IT WAS A FEW MINUTES BEFORE I REALIZED I WASN'T STILL PLAYING "RESIDENT EVIL"

aah...
Zombies! fight...

FEBRUARY 19, 2006

ICE DRAGONS

HUFF HAAAA

FEBRUARY 20, 2006

LAWRENCE BARNES

WE PLAYED A LITTLE ROCK-SHOW AT 8:30 IN THE MORNING FOR THE ELEMENTARY SCHOOL. AFTERWARDS I ANSWERED QUESTIONS:

ARE you famous?

Um... a little bit

Do you have any CDs?

Yeah... but they have swears on them.

FEBRUARY 21, 2006

AWESOME LETTERS

The kids wrote us thank-you notes for the rock show.

Here, I'll read 'em to ya.

"I've never seen an assembly like that before! When I heard that song my head rang like a bell of glory"

Or this one: "Fun! Cool! Awesome! Unique! Silly! Funny! Loud! Exciting! Fun to watch! I like it! ROBOT!"

ROBOT

FEBRUARY 22, 2006

SEXY PAJAMAS

What's the matter?

I don't like that sweatshirt you sleep in

Don't you have anything sexier?

You're an ass.

FEBRUARY 23, 2006

LIVING LIFE

I scared!

You're doing great

Excuse me... are you James Kochalka?

I hope you don't mind me asking

I got "superstarred" again, in the pool by a pretty mom

-that happens every where you go

What did she look like?

Oh...

like a pretty mom

FEBRUARY 24, 2005

MARDI GRAS EXCITEMENT

Eli...

Do you want to wake up and go watch Mommy in the parade?

sigh

FEBRUARY 25, 2006

...OUR PARADE

Woo! James KOCHALKA SUPERSTAR! AND ELI!!!

Did we miss the parade?

DRAG QUEEN

Oh, I'm afraid so...

fuck

But don't worry, James. You're YOUR OWN parade!

FEBRUARY 25, 2006

CANADIAN VACATION

Should I shave before we leave on our trip?

Well, you should at least shave your grumpies!

PART TWO

Today's strip is only two panels long.

Am I in it?

No.

Maybe you need a "Part Two"

FEBRUARY 26, 2006

GEORGIE'S GUESTS

BOUNCE

TOM & PEGGY'S BABY

THE RAMONES

I'm having a dance party with GEORGIE!

BOUNCE

I'm having a dance party with our clothes!

FOLD

FEBRUARY 27, 2006

TAP WATER

A LITTLE SIP AFTER BRUSHING OUR TEETH

Sssip!

MEMORIES

Boy the water was COLD in Canada.

what do you mean?

The tap water was very cold

Yeah, but... EVERYTHING is cold in Canada.

BACK HOME

FEBRUARY 28, 2006

CANADIAN MONSTER

What was your favorite part of our trip to Canada?

Going to the store

You mean when Daddy and Tom and Eli went to buy stuff to make dinner?

Yeah

The fondue?

But I thought you were a little bit scared of Tom.

Yes. He's a monster

Sweetheart, he's not a monster. He's just a grown-up with a beard.

oh

MARCH 1, 2006

HAIRCUT PORTRAITURE

oh!

Now draw mommy's haircut

Sit down, Mommy!

In a minute

Sit Down!

MARCH 2, 2006

HUMAN SUFFERING

Ooooh... whimper

What's the matter?

I want you...

Do you have a tummy-ache?

Yes

A Real tummy-ache or a pretend one?

Pretend

Oh No!

My little boy has a pretend tummy ache!

MARCH 3, 2006

CEILING

ABOVE THE GUEST BED AT MY PARENT'S HOUSE

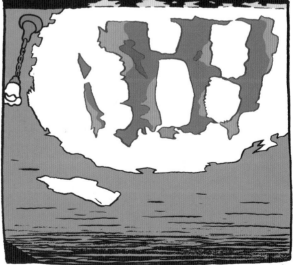

MARCH 4, 2006

PROUDLY NAPPING

I PUT ELI'S NEW LITTLE BED TOGETHER

I have scewdiver!

I helping

AND TOOK APART HIS CRIB

Look out!

KRACHAWNK

This will be your first nap in your new bed. Do you feel proud?

Yes

I'm proud of you, too

MARCH 8, 2006

SHHH

I SHOULD BE GETTING SOME WORK DONE.

...I WANT TO GET IN THAT COZY LITTLE BED, BUT I AM MUCH TOO BIG.

when's he gonna wake up?

MARCH 9, 2006

PERSISTENCE OF IGNORANCE

SPANDY HAS THROWN UP DOZENS OF TIMES ON OUR BEDROOM CARPET. I HATE IT.

WE'VE GOT TO TEAR IT UP. WHAT'S THE FLOOR LIKE UNDERNEATH?

PULL

I CAN'T TELL WHAT I'M LOOKING AT.

??

MARCH 10, 2006

QUACKY CAT

SNHUF

Uack!

Oh. I guess you're a duck now?

SALTY WATER

DRIP

A drop of rain just hit me in the mouth.

LICK

It's salty

MARCH 11, 2006

BLOGOSPHERE

WALKING HOME FROM JOSH BRIDGMAN'S "THE SILENT INVASION", I FEEL LIKE AN ACTOR IN A PLAY.

I DON'T SEE AN AUDIENCE...

BUT I KNOW THEY ARE OUT THERE.

MARCH 12, 2006

THE CARTOONIST'S BLACK BLOOD

DOING MY TAXES WITH A BRUSH & INDIA INK

DIP

DRAW

that looks nice

MARCH 13, 2006

I'VE BEEN WAITING ALL DAY FOR MY HOCKEY MONKEY EP TO GO LIVE ON ITUNES

WHERE IS IT?

LAST FALL I PUT A PIECE OF SCREEN OVER THE VENT THAT LEADS TO THE BATHROOM CEILING.

SO THIS SPRING THE BIRD CAME BACK AND BUILT HER LITTLE NEST UNDER THE EAVE ON THE FRONT PORCH

I KNOCKED IT DOWN WHILE SHE WATCHED.

Hockey Monkey?

MARCH 14, 2006

THEMESONG TO THE LOOP

MY SONG, HOCKEY MONKEY, IS ON T.V.

I wish there was a way I could float into homes across america and watch them watch the show

what?! They're just sitting there watching it.

COMMERCIAL BREAK

*Hockey Monkey to you, Hockey Monkey to you ♪

* TO THE TUNE OF "HAPPY BIRTHDAY"

MARCH 15, 2006

CUTE Li'L HANGOVER

Why did you wake up screaming?! You woke up Eli right as I was trying to get ready!

What? I was in pain...

I didn't mean to... Someone was tearing my arm off.

MARCH 16, 2006

UNSTOPABLE

So...

Is he going to play the song he sold to the devil?

HERE'S OUR $25,000 SONG, mutherfuckers!

SAINT PATRICK'S DAY   MARCH 17, 2006

LARS FISK

Maybe someday one of your sculptures can be the theme song to a T.V. show!

You're a cruel bastard.

HUG

CRUEL BASTARD

KISS

Ow

You sliced my cheek open with your FACE NEEDLES

MARCH 18, 2006

WINKED OUT

A COUPLE WEEKS AGO I SAW A BIRD.

IT DISAPPEARED IN A FLASH OF BLUE,

...THEN REAPPEARED AN INSTANT LATER.

I FORGOT TO DRAW ABOUT THIS UNTIL TODAY

MARCH 19, 2006

ILLUSION & FANTASY

ADVENTURES IN BUSINESS LUNCHING

This is going to be a 250 million dollar business!

As a creator you have a moral obligation to help me make this business succeed!

I need you to sign a Non-Disclosure Agreement

Huh? I missed a bunch of what you said. I was day-dreaming

MARCH 20, 2006

HEY, FAGGOT!

So... I got so emotional watching "V for Vendetta" that afterwards I told Tara a whole bunch of stuff that I went through in High School

But I called her back the next day and asked her to forget I ever said anything.

She said she would

It's not like anything that bad happened to me, it just causes me pain to think about that time.

I thought you were a CELEBRITY in High School.

I sort of was

MARCH 21, 2006

MONSTER HUNTERS

Do you see the dragon?

Eek!

Eek!

Spandy is a dragon!

Run!

MARCH 22, 2006

KITTY-POO

Hey!

The kitty put one of her poo-poos in my shoe!

Why would she do that?

Luckily it's hard and dry, though.

Kitty dried it?

I think it just dried naturally

MARCH 23, 2006

BOUNCY BED

MARCH 24, 2006

BIGGER

MARCH 25, 2006

PARENTING

MARCH 26, 2006

JOKE INVENTING

MARCH 27, 2006

GHOST TAX

A tax Refund?

I'm not owed a tax Refund, godamn it.

No good can come of this.

I think maybe my first estimated tax payment for 2006 was accidentally returned to me.

MARCH 28, 2006

FIRST PERSON SHOOTER

ON THE BUS TO THE CENTER FOR CARTOON STUDIES

oh god, I think I might actually throw up

Gotta get back to my spaceship...

Do you know what a FIRST-PERSON-Shooter is?

No.

MARCH 29, 2006

COLORS OF THE
GRASSY HILL

Everything is BROWN!

But soon enough it will be green

MARCH 30, 2006

WARMER WEATHER

Do all the boys look more handsome in the warmer weather?

I don't know

All the girls look beautiful!

Even the ugly ones!

"thank you"

MARCH 31, 2006

RAINY WATER

Stick your hand out the little window

mmm!

LICK

Rain is delicious!

APRIL 1, 2006

AIR NATIONAL GUARD

AMY'S BROTHER **LEFT** FOR IRAQ TODAY. LAST NIGHT WE HAD A GOING AWAY THING.

I'm going to see if I can find your base on Google's satellite map.

No... that won't work

You think it's censored? I bet I can do it.

What city is it near?

I'll look for an air-field nearby...

SOON: Look, bunkers! And that's definitely a military transport

Oh great! Now the FBI will come to my house

CLICK CLICK

APRIL 2, 2006

OVER THERE

OVERHEARD BY A PASSING GIRL ARE WE:

Look, it's the Bad Island

tee hee

That's where the monsters live.

APRIL 3, 2006

PALE IMITATION

SNOW FALLING FAST AND HARD IS **SPATIALLY DISORIENTING**

DIZZY, I WALK THE EDGE OF THE DIMENSIONAL RIFT.

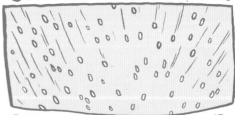

APRIL 4, 2006

(AFTER DRAWING THIS I GOT THE FEELING THAT MAYBE I HAD DRAWN THIS SAME STRIP BEFORE. LOOKING THROUGH THE FIRST BIG AMERICAN ELF COLLECTION, I FOUND IT: FEBRUARY 4, 2002 I DREW ALMOST EXACTLY THE SAME THING, BUT BETTER. AM I BECOMING A PALER AND PALER IMITATION OF MY OWN SELF? FUCK IT.)

THE BUS RIDER

IF THE UNIVERSE IS GOVERNED ENTIRELY BY PHYSICAL LAWS THEN FREE WILL IS IMPOSSIBLE. EVERY ATOM IS JUST FOLLOWING THE CAUSE AND EFFECT OF EVEN SMALLER SUBATOMIC FORCES.

HOWEVER, I THINK THE BRAIN MIGHT ACTUALLY BE MAGIC. I THINK PERHAPS IT TRANSCENDS THE LAWS OF PHYSICS.

I BELIEVE THAT OUR MINDS SHAPE AND DEFINE THE UNIVERSE AS WE MOVE THROUGH IT.

AND NOT JUST HUMAN MINDS, ANIMALS TOO. WE ARE ALL GODS, CREATING THE UNIVERSE IN WHICH WE LIVE.

APRIL 5, 2006

McMOTHER'S MILK

Mommy... I want to nurse

Honey, there's no milk in my breasts

I wan' McDonald's

APRIL 6, 2006

THE DATE

Before we go get Eli, I want to go to the drugstore and get more of those "CREATURE KIDS".

CRANK

Oh, I got another Ice-Bat guy

I've got $3.00 in quarters. I'm gonna try again

I'M A LITTLE BIT OBSESSED WITH THESE 25¢ KNOCK-OFFS OF THE UGLY-DOLLS.

APRIL 7, 2006

UP & DOWN

Stick my finger in the sky ♪♫

Stick your finger in the SKY ♪♫

Stick my finger in the poop ♫

ha ha

Happy happy happy happy ♪♫

Wow!

Happy yucky POOP! ♫

APRIL 8, 2006

HORNY STORIES

I'm going to the store. Do you want anything?

Get me something SEXY

You mean like hotdogs?

Are hotdogs sexy?

I guess they are like penises...

And you can stick them in your bun.

Ah!

APRIL 9, 2006

hot Sparkles!

APRIL 10, 2006

FIRST PORN

LAST NIGHT AT STEVE TREMBLEY'S PARTY

Mommy, look it yook it yook it yook it yook it yook it

CARDS

It's it's it's it's it's got LADIES

Eek!

APRIL 11, 2006

MY STUTTER BUG

Look here comes another little kid

oh!

You you you you you you you you you you ooo you you you ooo

You you you- you wanna play?

APRIL 12, 2006

DON'T WORRY

So, Eli's started stuttering?

Uh... yeah

But he's just joking, Right?

No, it's Real.

Oh... is it Really serious then?

um.. I don't think so

Don't worry daddy!

APRIL 13, 2006

MMM

Fine! I'll sleep on the COUCH theN!

LATER

I decided that instead of sleeping on the couch I'd come to bed and play with your boobies

mmm

APRIL 14, 2006

SHOWER TALK

There's No hot water

Where'd it go?

evapo-Rated?

I've got Some boiling water on the Stove...

Ah! That must be where it went

... I could dump it on you.

hee hee

APRIL 15, 2006

EASTER MORNING

Eli! Eli! Do you think the Easter Bunny came?

VROOOOM

I hear him!

APRIL 16, 2006

RUMBLING ENGINE

I'm cold.

Maybe I should drink another cup of coffee?

I'm NERVOUS about my trip TOMORROW.
SSIP

Maybe I should JERK off again?

AWAITING TAKE-OFF
APRIL 17, 2006

ON THE SET

OF "HOCKEYVILLE", PRACTICING HOCKEY MONKEY

I don't think I can sing the song as high as we recorded it.
YOU HAVE TO

Didn't we pitchshift my vocals?
Barely!
Come ON! You can do it

My ear things keep falling out!
They'll NEVER stay in

You've got to push them in deeper!
I'm dying!

KINGSTON, ONTARIO
APRIL 18, 2006

LET DOWN

THE ZAMBONIS AND I GAVE A SPECTACULAR PERFORMANCE TO A CROWD OF ABOUT 2000 PEOPLE

BUT ALL MY GREAT MOVES WERE EDITED OUT FOR TELEVISION, REPLACED BY VIDEOS OF LITTLE KIDS SKATING AROUND.

here it comes!

? Oh NOOO

KINGSTON, ONTARIO
APRIL 19, 2006

TWO FOREHEAD STORIES

TELEVISION FOREHEAD

PAT PAT

Probably my favorite part was when they put make-up on my bald spot! It was embarrassing
To make it less shiny?

FOREHEAD FRINGE

Why are you pulling on my bangs?
TUG TUG

To make them longer. I wish you didn't cut them.

APRIL 20, 2006

DOCTOR KOCHALKA

SPANDY HAD A BLACK SPOT ON HER SKIN THAT I WAS AFRAID MIGHT BE CANCER, BUT FOR THE LAST MONTH OR SO I HAVE CAREFULLY SCRATCHED AWAY AT IT...

Okay, Spandy.

You're CURED!

APRIL 21, 2006

ELI HELPED ME DRAW TODAY'S COMIC:

APRIL 22, 2006

PAIN

Stop daddy

Stop

I'm just trying to see if YOUR arm is broken.

No

Poke

& PLEASURE

IS that cashew-butter ON YOUR pants, OR poo poo?

Cashew butter

Good... 'cause I just ate some.

APRIL 23, 2006

X-RAY

HOW is Eli?

He broke his collar bone at the "family gym"

I mean REALLY broke it...

Like this!

APRIL 24, 2006

MONSTER DREAMS

Panel 1: I I dream I dream about a little monster a little monster named Agga!

Panel 2: Daddy dream that Jason tried to kiss mommy!

You did?

Panel 3: No, I did. A few weeks ago.

And I think it was Alan

Yeah!

APRIL 25, 2006

SPRING CLEANING

Panel 1: Look Colby, I don't have a bald spot anymore!

Panel 2: It's cat hair

Panel 3: That's disgusting. You were grooming the cat?

Yeah, we shampooed the carpet too.

Panel 4: But we're thinking of just replacing it with a cat-puke colored carpet.

APRIL 26, 2006

PENNY MONSTER

Panel 1: That pine tree looks like the Penny Monster.*

Panel 2: And look! Little baby Penny Monsters

Do you want to give one a penny?

Yeah

Panel 3: Give it to that one

Panel 4: Oops. He dropped it.

I missed!

* FROM THE BEDTIME STORIES I TELL

APRIL 27, 2006

SUNSHINE ON THE DIARIST

Panel 2: I want to PUNCH someone.

Panel 4: SKRITCH SKETCH SKETCH

APRIL 28, 2006

MAPLE FESTIVAL CAR WASH

Boys?! Yuck. I would ONLY get my car washed by college girls.

What about High-School girls?

Oh sure, High-School girls, too.

They're college-girls-in-training

APRIL 29, 2006

MAPLE URINE FESTIVAL

Snif Snif

My pee is MAPLE SYRUP!

APRIL 29, 2006

SATURDAY NIGHT FIRE BOMB

SOMEONE FIRE-BOMBED THE NEXT-DOOR NEIGHBOR'S CAR

APRIL 30, 2006

IN MY HEAD, IN MY BED

LATELY, I'VE BEEN USING PERSONAL CORRESPONDENCE FROM OTHER CARTOONISTS AS BOOKMARKS.

AND, I USED ONE FROM JOHN PORCELLINO** AS A BOOKMARK WHILE READING "THE FATE OF THE ARTIST" BY EDDIE CAMPBELL.

I USED A LETTER FROM THE YOUNG T. EDWARD BAK* WHILE READING "SCULPTOR'S DAUGHTER" BY TOVE JANSSON. (WHICH I GOT ON INTER-LIBRARY LOAN).

ART AND ARTISTS INTERSECTING BY CHANCE, IN MY HEAD AND IN MY BED.

* AUTHOR OF "SERVICE INDUSTRY"
** AUTHOR OF "KING-CAT"

MAY 1, 2006

TEXAS RAIN

THEY FLEW ME DOWN FOR A BIG "FREE COMIC BOOK DAY" EVENT. HERE, UNDER A BIG TENT IN THE

Rain! Does this mean the show's over? What time is it?

There's still three more hours to go.

And now it's stopping. Well... as far as I'm concerned that's the EMOTIONAL end of the event.

ZEUS COMICS, DALLAS, TX   MAY 6, 2006

FANCY GLASS

AFTERPARTY FOR "CAPE" WITH LIVE ART & DJ IN A FANCY BAR WITH FANCY PEOPLE.

This beer tastes good with the mint gum in my mouth.

And the bar-tender girl called me "baby"

AND THEN DRUNKENLY PAINTING A STACK OF PAC-MAN GHOSTS

DALLAS, TX   MAY 7, 2006

WAITING FOR THE POP

I'VE GOT A PLANE STUCK IN MY EAR.

OR A LITTLE BIT OF CLOUD.

I'VE GOT A CASE OF AIRPLANE HEAD

MAY 8, 2006

RUSTY NOOSE

A HOOP OF RUSTY METAL, LONG EMBEDDED IN THE TREE

CREAK CRACK

MAY 9, 2006

UNPOPPABLE

My ear still hasn't popped

Amy suggested I have a shot of whiskey but it didn't help.

Did you pour it in your ear?
No
Try it.

MAY 10, 2006

SUPER POWER

Sspchoo

WUMP
TRIP

My powers!

Waaa! My powers gone!

MAY 11, 2006

MAYBE IVY

BACK OF MY NECK

Does that look like poison ivy?

Nm... it could be
maybe

My whole life I've been afraid of getting poison ivy
maybe I finally did it

MAY 12, 2006

THE ARTIST

What are you mad about?

Eli said he doesn't want to draw with me.

Eli, if you draw with daddy when we get home, you can have a cookie
Okay!

Can I have a cookie too?

MAY 13, 2006

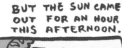
GRASS FLUFFER

IT'S BEEN RAINING HARD FOR DAYS...

BUT THE SUN CAME OUT FOR AN HOUR THIS AFTERNOON.

I FLUFFED UP THE NEW BABY GRASS THAT HAD BEEN SQUASHED AND FLATTENED BY THE RAIN.

FLUFF FLUFF

MAY 18, 2006

GOOD MORNING

Time to get up, James.

okay

Daddy! YOUR PENIS Standing UP!

Uh, Yeah...

Push it back DOWN, Daddy

MAY 19, 2006

THESE TWO DUDES

Look, there's Colin

Hey baby!

SLAP

Now that I'm famous, I call everyone "baby".

You should wear dark glasses!

MAY 20, 2006

TIPSY GENIUS

AAH!

IN typical genius fashion, I dipped my whiteout brush in the india ink.

Is that because you had 2 beers at dinner?

No, it's because I'm a genius

MAY 21, 2006

PISTOL

MY GOOD FRIEND PISTOL IS BACK IN TOWN FOR A REUNION SHOW WITH HIS OLD BAND, THE PANTS

I'm so excited to see you, I'm hyperventilating

So, will you draw me in your strip?

Don't say that!

Stop saying that!

WE WENT TO VISIT JASON AT HIS WORK & EAT THERE AND JASON SAT DOWN WITH US

Dude, he NEVER draws about me anymore

I know! I'm sorry!

MAY 22, 2006

ELI DREW HIS FIRST COMIC BOOK AND I JUST GOT BACK FROM PHOTOCOPYING IT AT KINKO'S

first you fold the papers carefully

Then we staple it.

KACHUNK

Then stamp it with the "Kochalka Quality" logo.

And there's your very first book! Do you like it?

Do you want to read it?

Do you like it?

MAY 23, 2006

SAVE THE WORMS

AFTER A LONG WET SPELL, FINALLY TODAY IS SUNNY. BUT A WEEK AGO I WAS A BIG HERO IN THE RAIN:

A worm is drowning

You saved it?

Daddy saved the worm!

MAY 24, 2006

WOOD NYMPH

COLBY HAD A TREE CUTTING PARTY

CRASH

BZWAA

I'm lusting after that wood.

Colby, I'm lusting to burn your tree in my wood stove

You can have it!

Happy birthday

MAY 24, 2006

ERASER GHOST

RUB RUB

I erase you, daddy

It's like I'm not even here.

MAY 25, 2006

B-NAP

I'm barely reeeeading...

Oh who cares

Z

RING

HAPPY BIRTHDAY

You woke me up from my birthday nap

MAY 26, 2006

DRUNK PHOENIX

Tingling

My head's on fire!

This can't be real...

Oh God it burns

(AFTER MY BIRTHDAY ROCK SHOW 3:00 AM)

MAY 27, 2006

GLORY

LAST NIGHT AT THE PANTS' REUNION SHOW I GAVE AN IMPROMPTU CONCERT IN THE MEN'S BATHROOM:

Doing whippits in triplet and spittin' out blood ♪

I did No-doze with Slow Dog til he punched me in the gut ♪

And I siphoned more gas than I'm ever gonna huff ♫

but when you live in the North End you gotta stay tough! ♫

Yeah!

NORTH END

MAY 28, 2006

FRY ROUTINE

Rachel, check it out. First you dip the French fry in ketchup.

and the French fry says "Do you like my red hair?"

Yes, I like your red hair.

Chomp

"Thanks for the haircut!"

MAY 29, 2006

PINK TRIANGLE

SPANDY'S EAR GOT TURNED INSIDE OUT

MAKING A PINK TRIANGLE

Ha ha. Your ear is "gay".

MAY 30, 2006

LITTLE VOID

What's this

Tree seeds

See, there's little seeds inside each one.

I'll open it up and show you.

Hey. It's empty!

MAY 31, 2006

ABORTION

INDIA INK, HAIR, & MILDEW BUILD UP, DOWN THE DRAIN

SHLORP

Amy look what I found in the drain!

Why are you showing me this?

Because you want to see it

JUNE 1, 2006

CAT HAIR GLIDER

JUNE 2, 2006

ANOMALY

IN 1985 OR 1986 MY COLLEGE RADIO STATION GOT THIS RECORD BY GUY GOODE & THE DECENTONES.

Oh my God! I need this

IT BECAME ONE OF MY FAVORITE RECORDS OF ALL TIME.

Take one! They sent us FIVE copies for some reason

Wow

YESTERDAY, ON MY WAY TO WATCH "THE DEVIL & DANIEL JOHNSTON" I GOT A PACKAGE FROM THE SISTER OF ONE OF THE GUYS IN THE BAND. I TOOK THE PACKAGE TO THE MOVIE.

SHE HAD READ AN INTERVIEW WHERE I MENTIONED MY LOVE FOR THE BAND AND SENT ME SIX CDs OF MORE OF HER BROTHER'S MUSIC.*

* ALMOST UNLISTENABLE!

JUNE 3, 2006

BEACH TOOTH

Look, my tooth fell out

Do you still have that tooth-shaped rock?

I threw it in the lake

Oh... I wanted to draw it.

Don't worry. It will wash back up on the beach in a hundred years

JUNE 4, 2006

TO BE CONTINUED..?

LEAF EAR

I didn't get my food

I know, honey

It's because the waitress forgot to bring our food

She made me very angry

PLUCK

?

Don't put a LEAF in my EAR!

JUNE 5, 2006

POISONOUS BOY

JUNE 6, 2006

ANTI-POWERS

JUNE 7, 2006

BAGLE LICKER

JUNE 8, 2006

FREEDOM

JUNE 9, 2006

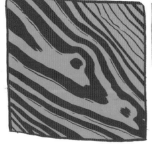

HAWKMAN & HOT MILK

I want my mommy

Mommy's at the Boston Aquarium, remember? She slept in the jellyfish-room last night.

Do you want to play with your new Hawkman toy?

Yes, and hot milk

SOON

Suck suck suck

JUNE 10, 2006

ZOMBIES & ANGELS

Eli, let's change your diaper.

No!

I'm dead

Well, I guess there's no reason to change a dead boy's diaper.

What?! But we don't want him to smell all poopy at the funeral!

JUNE 11, 2006

FLOORS & CEILINGS

IN MY HOUSE

JUNE 12, 2006

THE END

click

He doesn't see me...

Oh... is that a gun?

Amy... the neighbor just turned and pointed a gun right at my face.

JUNE 13, 2006

COME WITH ME

?!?

That can't be what time it is.

What the fuck? Am I dead? Why is time all messed up today? Did my neighbor actually blow my brains out last night?*

Eli! Come with me!

* SEE YESTERDAY'S STRIP

JUNE 14, 2006

BARBQUE UMBRELLA

plit

...It just started Raining...

Oh... I can cook the chicken inside then

No!

I want to BARBECUE

JUNE 15, 2006

EVERYTHING...

Time to change your diaper. It's all pee-pee

No! We have to

Waaa! That was my SPECIAL pee-pee

Put it back!

...IS SPECIAL

You made a poo-poo. Can I change your diaper?

No. It's special to me.

They're ALL special

JUNE 16, 2006

THE NEIGHBOR

CLANG CLANG CLANG CLANG

James

He's on the Roof!

JUNE 17, 2006

GREATEST DAD 2006

APOLOGIZING TO AMY

I'm SORRY I was so grouchy today.

I don't do well with "special" days

I like the shirt & pants & socks, though

Greatest DAD

APOLOGIZING TO ELI:

I'm SORRY I was so persnickety today.

I still had lots of fun with you, though

FATHER'S DAY

JUNE 18, 2006

PAPER TOWEL

THE SKY HUNG LOW LIKE A WET PAPER TOWEL ABOUT TO SPLIT OPEN FROM THE WEIGHT.

AND... THEN IT DOES:

JUNE 19, 2006

MY EMMY AWARD

TODAY IS THE LAST DAY OF NOMINATIONS FOR THE 2006 EMMY AWARDS

But I really really WANT to win an Emmy for Hockey Monkey

Oh... Right. It's like ten years old. Of course it's NOT eligible.

96

Well... I'll just PRETEND I WON an Emmy, then.

Eli... will you be my little Emmy award?

No!

I just want to be Eli

JUNE 20, 2006

ICE CREAM CHUCKER

If you're all done with your ice-cream, you can throw it down the bank.

for the worms?

And the skunks and the squirrels

Now we'll brush your teeth & get ready for nap time

Ugh

I ate it all up.

Well, some of it. You threw the REST down the bank

JUNE 21, 2006

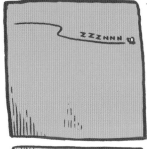
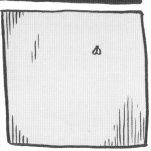

MAGIC ON THE BUS

"I'd like to be a magician's assistant. Do you know any magicians?"

"No... but I know some people I would assist if they were."

"But what I REALLY want is to be in a basket and have swords stuck through it and survive."

"She's touching my body **"

DROOL Zz

JUNE 26, 2006

* "MAGIC FOR BEGINNERS" BY KELLY LINK
** JUST A LITTLE BIT, AS THE BUS TURNS

KNOCK KNOCK

"Hello" "Hi"

"I live just down the street."

"So... I hear our neighbor has a new "appliance"."

"Oh, um"

"uh"

"I read your strip in Seven Days. *"

"Yeah"

"I geuss he's got a gun"

"You don't think he reads the strip too, do you?"

* THE LOCAL PAPER THAT RUNS THIS STRIP

JUNE 27, 2006

BEST FRENZY

"That Daddy's best friend."

LATER

MOSQUITTO!

SLAP

"Yuck! I got your aids-blood all over my hand."

"Hey!"

JUNE 28, 2006

TIRED WINGS GLIDE HIGH

I'M SOO TIRED FROM OUR ROCK SHOW IN MONTREAL LAST NIGHT,

BUT THIS TIRED FEELS REAL GOOD LIKE A THICK & MELLOW HIGH.

"I love you Eli"

AND SO I GET A SURPRISE DELIVERY: ONE THOUSAND COPIES OF MY NEW CD, SPREAD YOUR EVIL WINGS AND FLY*

!!!!!

"I'm high-fiving you over the phone!"

* NOT DUE IN STORES TIL SEPT. 12

JUNE 29, 2006

MINI B·B·Q

PULLING INTO OUR DRIVEWAY AFTER KERRIE & RYAN'S BIRTHDAY PARTY

 Don't hit the little Robot.

It's our little friend who makes us dinner

JUNE 30, 2006

IN THE DRINK

 We drink in the winter to numb the pain and drink in the summer to celebrate life.

 We drink in the fall to acknowledge the passage of time...

And in the spring we... um... in the spring we drink to anticipate ...um... to

in the spring we toast the flowers

JULY 1, 2006

SUPER CROQUET

 .....

I tie you up!

KLONK

 but I blast you with my BLASTER HAMMER!

ARG!

JULY 2, 2006

SPARKLE BURN

WATCHING THE FIREWORKS UPSIDE DOWN,

SUNBURNED WHERE I COULDN'T REACH

WITH THE SUNSCREEN. JULY 3, 2006

REMOTE

We can't watch a movie. The batteries are dead in the remote control!!!

Let's watch a movie!

The battery is dead, remember?

Well, we've got new batteries but it still won't work!

I guess we need a new T.V.

Mommy went to buy some! We have to wait till she gets back, remember?

JULY 4, 2006

LUVERZ

Do you still want to make love to me tonight?

But you've been mean to me today.

What!? No I haven't

You haven't?

Then why am I punishing you?

(LAST NIGHT)

JULY 5, 2006

DARTH VADAR

SUDDENLY WE'RE IN WEST VIRGINIA AT THE RACE TRACK *

Kate, "Knock Knock"

Who's there?

Darth

Darth who?

GESUNDHEIT!

FOOD COURT MINOTAUR

No children are allowed in the casino

I'm hungry

You must leave at once

But there's no way out of this maze

* WE LOST $2 ON A HORSE CALLED "ONE SHARP SWORD"

JULY 6, 2006

NATURAL VIRTUE

THE GATE AT THE "HILLTOP HOUSE", OVER-LOOKING THE POTOMAC, WHICH WE ARE PRETENDING IS A VIDEO GAME

where do you put the quarter in?

Right here

what's this game called?

Mr. Blinky

HARPER'S FERRY WEST VIRGINIA

JULY 7, 2006

CHESS MASTERS

"I launch my Rocket!"

"Hi"

HILLTOP HOUSE HOTEL — JULY 8, 2006

GLITTER IN MY EYE

CARRYING SOME FANCY WEDDING PRESENTS FOR JESSE & CUPCAKE UP FROM THE CAR JUST IN CASE PRETTY PRESENTS ARE TOO ENTICING FOR THE CRIMINALS TO RESIST.

THUMP

CHECK

BLINK

SLIP

WIPE

WASHINGTON, DC
DURING FINAL GAME OF WORLD CUP — JULY 9, 2006

(THE PAINTING'S CALLED "STAR FALL")

ANSELM KIEFER

him fall down

AT THE HIRSHHORN — JULY 10, 2006

WASHINGTON, D.C.

I bought this Shirt like 25 years ago...

...and it's still the most expensive shirt I ever bought.

I think it was 40 or 60 bucks

where did you get it?

Washington, D.C.

Is that why you always wear it when we come here?

Yes

KATE & CHRIS' LITTLE ELEVATOR — JULY 10, 2006

SHITSTORM

Fuck it! I'm just going to try and squeeze as hard as I can!!
Ooh kay

NNNNG!

PLOOP

I made a poop the size of a PEA!

WASHINGTON, D.C.

JULY 11, 2006

EEK

ITALIA

whee Tee hee!
Here come your girlfriends again

!?..they're a little young for me...

giggle!
whee!
That's why you need two.

LATE LAST NIGHT IN A DULLES AIRPORT TOY STORE

JULY 12, 2006

LI'L DRUG BAG

MY BACK YARD

Hey look! It's one of those little drug packages!

Yup, it sure is.

It must've blown loose when our neighbor was EVICTED!!
HOoRAY!

JULY 13, 2006

SIBLING RIVALRY

Hisss!

Spandy hissed at me

Don't hiss at Eli, he's your brother

Spandy, I'm your bRother

JULY 14, 2006

DAVID ZACHARIS' BIRTHDAY EVENT

Can you feel the "Dave"?

Yes... but I am the Dave

JULY 14, 2006

A BIRD IS HERE

Are it's little feet stuck in the screen?
TAP TAP

JULY 15, 2006

FUZZY SURPRISE

WeeOo!

There's a fuzzy little groundhoggy little creature guy living under our porch.

So? Did it bite you?

JULY 16, 2006

RUM TUM TUM

This is just for grown ups. It's an alcohol drink.
I want it

No honey, it makes kids sick.

It'll make you throw up.

You like it?
Oh, I love it
I want some

JULY 17, 2006

IMPORTANT

THE MOST IMPORTANT THING TO BRING WHEN YOU GO ON A TRIP

IS EMERGENCY BACK-UP DISCS OF YOUR ARTWORK

JUST IN CASE SOMEONE BREAKS IN AND STEALS YOUR COMPUTER, OR THE HOUSE BURNS DOWN WHILE YOU'RE GONE.

JULY 18, 2006

SNAKES ON A PLANE

STARRING ELI KOCHALKA AS SAMUEL JACKSON

Snakes on the airplane! Snakes on the airplane!

I pooped! On the plane? POOP ON A PLANE! POOP ON A PLANE! Shhh!

JULY 19, 2006

LITTLE ANT BOOBIES

Amy! I just saw down a pretty girl's shirt from fifteen stories up

SAN DIEGO HYATT   JULY 20, 2006

HARD SELLER

I love your books!! !! Well then, you should buy my new CD.

Oh... um, I don't know... Oh, you'll buy it, all right! Ha Ha HAHA HA!

SAN DIEGO COMICON   JULY 21, 2006

WOKEN UP BY A PARTY DOWN THE HALL AT 3:00 AM
✱ JOHN LAYMAN'S PARTY

Oh... I've still got to draw my comic strip... but... ... ZZz

LATER

BLAM BLAM BLAH BLAM BLAH BLAM BLAH BLAM BLAH

wha?

SOON, AT THE PARTY

Oh gosh! Please, please everyone quiet down

Fuck you, Hitler!

SAN DIEGO COMICON, HYATT HOTEL JULY 22, 2006
✱ SOME GUY I DON'T KNOW

PUBLIC YELLING

LAST DAY OF THE COMIC-CON

COMICON!

COMICON!

COMICON! COMICON!!

COMICON!

SAN DIEGO, CA   JULY 23, 2006

AMUSING OURSELVES IN THE AIRPORT

I think I'll use the men's room.

I am feeling pretty manly today

MEN

C 10 FRANKFURT

We can come back here for a hotdog if we get hungry

C 10 FRANKFURT

CHICAGO O'HARE   JULY 24, 2006

MAGIC MONEY

DURING MY Q&A AT THE SAN DIEGO COMIC-CON, I TOLD A FUNNY STORY ABOUT HOW WE COULDN'T RECORD A NEW PUNKY BREWSKIES ALBUM BECAUSE JASON DIDN'T HAVE $125 FOR A NEW HARDDRIVE:

AFTER THE TALK (A COUPLE DAYS AGO)

Here, tell Jason that he sucks

okay!

$125!!

TODAY, AT JASON'S WORK (A COUPLE DAYS LATER)

So, this guy said to give you this money for a new harddrive so we could record a new Punky Brewskies album.

$ $

I knew I was waiting for something.

waiting for magic to happen

$ $

JULY 25, 2006

REMAINS OF MY DAY

girls in bikinis at the beach

9-11 conspiracy theories on the internet

annoying Amy

diary comics

JULY 26, 2006

LILYPAD FLOWERS

I'm going to pick another flower for the Moms.

No!

Don't! Don't!

Gee! How come you're so scared of flowers Turner?

I'm scared of flipping over!

JULY 27, 2006

DRIVING RAIN

I just pulled over because I can't see and I was panicking!

Why don't YOU drive if you have a problem with that!

No way. I would panic even under normal driving conditions

JULY 28, 2006

LONG LIVE KOCHALKA

MY PARENTS ARE GETTING SUPER OLD SO WE ALL GOT TOGETHER AND BURNED A BUNCH OF THEIR STUFF.

what about this?

BURN IT!

If any Trolls come, I'll poke 'em in the eye

PATRICK

"No Trespassing"?

So stay away "Grandpa"!

NO TRESPASSING

JULY 29, 2006

SMALL COMFORT

I'M HOME WITHOUT AMY & ELI FOR A COUPLE DAYS

the Indian food is warm against my lower back.

JULY 30, 2006

SAAG TOOTHPASTE

LEFTOVER CHICKEN SAAG

Spicy

I'll go work on that painting now... whoops! Can't forget to brush my teeth.

Wow! That's intense

CURRY & MINT —————— JULY 31, 2006

THE CAPTAIN

THE OTHER DAY I FOUND THIS PAINTING OF A PILOT IN THE ROYAL AIR FORCE OR SOMETHING WHILE CLEANING OUT MY PARENT'S GARAGE.

BUT LATER, MY SISTER PUT A HOLE THROUGH IT.

Wow! That's pretty darn good!

I ripped that painting you liked.

What!?

Nooo

IT DOESN'T ACTUALLY EVEN BELONG TO MY FOLKS... THEY WERE JUST HOLDING ON TO IT FOR A FRIEND.

AND THIS IS HOW I FIXED IT.

Don't worry, Mom. I can fix it

AUGUST 1, 2006

SUPER HUMID

I BUILT A NEW WINDOW-SILL OUT OF SCRAPS & "WOOD FILLER".

WENT TO DECLAN'S BIRTHDAY PARTY AT NORTH BEACH.

Minnows! We can have minnow sandwiches for lunch

RODE HOME FROM THE BEACH IN THE POURING RAIN.

AUGUST 2, 2006

HORNY

Look

She wants me to fuck that hole in the tree

Our tree has a belly button!

AUGUST 3, 2006

SPOTS OF ROT

KEEP FINDING NEW SPOTS OF ROT.

SOFT WOOD HOLDS WATER LIKE A SPONGE AND CRUMBLES TO JUICY WET FLAKES UPON DISCOVERY.

I DON'T WANT TO REPLACE THEM BUT I CAN'T FIGHT THE ROT ANYMORE. AFRAID ANY NEW WINDOW WILL BE AN UGLY MONSTROSITY. WENT TO SEE "A SCANNER DARKLY" BUT CAN'T STOP THINKING ABOUT ROTTEN WINDOWS THROUGHOUT MOST OF THE MOVIE.

AUGUST 4, 2006

UNIVERSAL REVERSAL

I RODE AMY'S BIKE AND SHE RODE MINE

Amy! Your bike feels so different from mine

I don't even know what's REAL anymore

AUGUST 5, 2006

ALMOST THREE

When you were first born, I was SO scared...

...because I had never taken care of a baby before.

But then you taught me how to be a daddy.

AUGUST 6, 2006

AWAKE

FIRST THING THIS MORNING, ELI WENT DOWNSTAIRS ALONE.

Eli?

Go away.

I told you Momma would be gone for a couple days...

Go AWAY! DON'T WANT YOU!

AUGUST 7, 2006

SALT WATER

Tomorrow we'll get mommy and go to the ocean.

And what will we do at the ocean..?

..with our tongues?

Taste it!

AUGUST 8, 2006

LAWNMOWER FAIRIES

Hey Garth, hear that sound?

Every couple weeks this summer, these guys show up and mow our lawn.

But we didn't hire them. They're coming by mistake!

BVVVVVV

It's awesome!

AUGUST 9, 2006

SQUISHY SCITUATE

SQUISH

HEY ELI

what

Something SQUISHIE happened to my feet!

SCITUATE, MASS.

AUGUST 10, 2006

PEE DANCER

Do you have to pee? Run to the potty.

No

I like to pee on the porch

BEACH HOUSE

AUGUST 11, 2006

SHORTSQUAD

Nobody likes my little shorts

I do, Tom!

SCITUATE, MASS.

AUGUST 11, 2006

BROOKE'S FAMILY BEACHOUSE

SCITUATE, MASS   AUGUST 12, 2006

FAMILY OF THREE

OUR blueberry plant made three blueberries.

A big one for Daddy...

A medium one for Mommy...

And a little one for Eli!

Let's get mommy and eat them together.

That's a good idea!

AUGUST 13, 2006

PRIMER

The eaves will be real pretty for when the birds come back to roost next spring

AUGUST 14, 2006

THE NEXT LAYER

My chest hurts. I don't feel good.

Maybe it's a heart attack

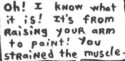

Oh! I know what it is! It's from raising your arm to paint! You strained the muscle.

That's IT!

Just one more layer after this

AUGUST 15, 2006

(I WROTE THIS COMIC STRIP IN A DREAM)

TODAY'S STRIP

AUGUST 16, 2006

RADIO INTERVIEW

AUGUST 17, 2006

EMMENTALER SUPERSTAR

NEW ORLEANS

AUGUST 18, 2006

CROTCH

I've got some bad crotch-chafing going on

I need to be dusted down with constarch like Rob Zombie

You should go into one of the strip clubs and ask for some "Lap Powder"

Do you think the girls really ride bicycles in there?

NEW ORLEANS

AUGUST 19, 2006

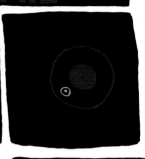
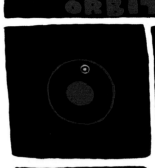

ORBITAL

Zz

How long have I been in orbit around this little planet?

AUGUST 20, 2006

ELI'S BIRTHDAY PARTY YESTERDAY WAS

CACOPHONOUS

I'm gonna go take a nap

Yeah, thanks for your help.

oh, fine

AUGUST 21, 2006

OLD NORTH END

VIDEO BANDIT

What are you gonna do with our VCR?

I'm borrowing it to make a music video

TURNER

I'm going to play the "GameBoy Camera" through the "GameBoy Player" through the "GameCube" to record it on the VCR.

??!!

WALKING HOME

Hey! There goes the VCR BANDIT!

AUGUST 22, 2006

BOSTON PHILLY NYC

Hey Neil... do we have places to sleep-over when we go on this mini-tour?

'Cause if we don't...

...YOU'RE gonna have to work hard to pick up girls in each city and get them to bring you home

And then say "um... can James come along too?"

AUGUST 23, 2006

LEAVES OF GRASS

GRAB

GRASS POWER!

TOSS

Grass power?

tee hee

GRASS POWER!

AUGUST 24, 2006

DRAWING THE STRIP ON TOUR

BRILLIANT SAYINGS

Wait. What'd you just say? I forgot what you said.

I don't remember

Fuck. My strip is ruined then

You did have a look on your face like I had just said something really brilliant.

"THE MIDDLE EAST"
CAMBRIDGE, MA

AUGUST 25, 2006

SNOW ROCK

I HAD A DREAM ABOUT PLAYING A ROCK SHOW IN A SNOW STORM.

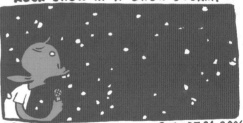

CAMBRIDGE, MA

AUGUST 26, 2006

A PLACE TO STAY

NEIL HAD KEYS TO SOME DUDE'S HOUSE

Gah! I'd rather stay awake all night than sleep here!!

What's that smell?

Look! Look! A dead mouse!

PHILADELPHIA, PA

AUGUST 26, 2006

NO LIQUIDS

AaRg!

I almost didn't even bring my ink...because of the "terror levels"

But... of course we didn't fly.

But then it exploded! So... there ya go.

HAPPENED IN PHILLY
DRAWN IN NYC

AUGUST 27, 2006

MEETING JAMES KOCHALKA

AT MY ROCK SHOW AT CAKE SHOP IN NYC

These kids are awesome
Oh Wow! Oh wow! You're awesome

Hi... I'm Phoebe Cates. Their mother.
Pretty!

Phoebe Kates. Phoebe Kates. Who is Phoebe Kates?

She's the one from Fast Times at Ridgemont High

NEW YORK CITY

AUGUST 27, 2006

LINGERING BUZZ

Thanks for booking the shows & everything, Neil. It was like a NON-STOP party! What an awesome little Rock tour.

BROOKLYN?

I even have two drink tickets left over from last night.
Quick!
Back to "Cake" shop"

AUGUST 28, 2006

OBSERVATIONAL COMEDY

That man is looking at me.

AUGUST 29, 2006

NEWMAN'S OWN™ COMIX

That's Paul Newman

Paul Newman is a tiny little monster...

Oh!

You took his head off!!

SEPTEMBER 3, 2006

COLD BREAKFAST TECH SUPPORT

No. I already did that. Yeah... okay. No.

Breakfast is Ready!
CAN'T!

Aaah... I guess I'll do it again. Uh... Nothing.

VERIZON

SEPTEMBER 4, 2006

WASH YOUR ASS
AWESOME ROCK VIDEO SHOOT

Dude... you got a huge WELT where that mosquito bit you.
Aah!

I'll cover it with suds

SEPTEMBER 5, 2006

CRANKY

I'm CRANKY!

Don't worry, Daddy. It'll be okay

Don't worry.

SEPTEMBER 6, 2006

WHEN COLIN CALLS

Colin... talking to you Reminds me that I'm wasting time. I gotta go.

Awesome.

HAPPY DAY

Poor Eli... are you sick? Poor little guy...

I'm Annakin Skywalker

SEPTEMBER 7, 2006

ANGRY MAD

The little hairs stand up when my arm swings

DRAWN DRUNKISH

SEPTEMBER 8, 2006

SWASHBUCKLER

Momma..?

I wish my PENIS was a SWORD.

SEPTEMBER 9, 2006

REALITY CHECK

You used to say So many funny things in my comic STRIP ...but it's been a while.

maybe I've been busy

SWEET NOTHINGS

You've got paint chips in your eyes

I was just about to say the same thing about you!

SEPTEMBER 10, 2006

SEPT. 11

IMAGINE TERRORISTS HIGH-JACKING THE BUS AND DRIVING IT INTO THE TOWERS.

SEPTEMBER 11, 2006

SPREAD YOUR EVIL WINGS & FLY

I feel weird today

Oh. That's too bad. Do you feel sick?

No... I just feel weird cause our new album came out today and I have no idea if anyone's gonna buy it or not...

SEPTEMBER 12, 2006

DREAM OF THE BAD MAN

There was a bad man in the house and he picked me up and it was scary

And he was wearing a pirate shirt.

You mean a skull shirt...like the one daddy has?

Yes

I think this dream was secretly about ME.

SEPTEMBER 13, 2006

CLIMBING INTO BED

Yuck!

I stepped on something cold and clammy.

Was that cat puke? Or some loose change?

SEPT. 14, 2006

101 JUSTIN TIMBERLAKES

The ReSeaRch department at SPIN wants to know how many times we say "Justin Timberlake" in that SONG.

Can you count it?

LATER Actually, fuck them. It's stupid.

It doesn't matter.

This is the last STRAW. I QUIT THE BAND! This is so beneath me.

Ha ha! You CAN'T quit the band.

Goodnight, Jason.

Ha ha

Yeah? Laugh yourself to sleep, faggot

(HE COUNTED 101)

SEPTEMBER 15, 2006

I have to tell you something.

?

I'm PReGNaNT.

wee hee hee!

FLOP

SEPTEMBER 16, 2006

HELLO!

Oh my God! Congratulations!

Thanks! It's a bit of a surprise since we weren't even trying...

-plus Amy was on the pill

Eeee!

SEPTEMBER 17, 2006

ELI, SICK IN BED

I'm poking your elbow

Poke Poke

Poke

Now I want to poke your other elbow.

SEPTEMBER 18, 2006

WUMP & JUMP

SEPTEMBER 19, 2006

PUMP DUCK

SEPTEMBER 20, 2006

ROCK THE PHONE

I CALLED ALL THE COLLEGE RADIO STATIONS THAT PLAYED MY NEW CD AND SANG THEM THANK-YOUS

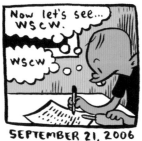

SEPTEMBER 21, 2006

50 OR 60 STATIONS!

STACKS OF FUN

SEPTEMBER 22, 2006

KAW

KAW KAW!

That CROW is laughing at my bottom!

SEPTEMBER 23, 2006

CATS LOVE CANS

Silly kitty, it's Mock Duck, not Real duck.

Meow

That's Right, Spandy... we're just mocking you.

meow

"if it comes from a can, I like it"

Meow!!

SEPTEMBER 24, 2006

LAWYER

Amy, are you divorcing me?

No!

Some lawyer said you called him... but he didn't know why...

I did dial a WRONG NUMBER this weekend but I hung up.

He must be desperate!

"A WRONG NUMBER? I'll TAKE THE CASE!"

SEPTEMBER 25, 2006

BUG DRUG

DEAD BUGS STUCK IN GRAY ENAMEL PAINT

They sure seem to love that stuff

SEPTEMBER 26, 2006

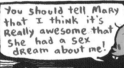

FATAL FLAWS

ELI SAT IN ON DRUMS WITH CHRIS & SASHA'S BAND

Man! He Needs to PRACTICE.

What? Come ON

(LAST NIGHT)

But he used to go WILD. He was CONCENTRATING ON the KICK DRUM

OCTOBER 1, 2006

MRS. SUPERSTAR

AMY'S FIRST DOCTOR'S APPOINTMENT OF THE PREGNANCY

And your husband is James Kahalla? Kochalaka... Ka..

"Kochalka."

Oh, yes. That's Right... the famous Rock Star.

OCTOBER 2, 2006

CRUSH ME

SINCE ELI WAS LITTLE BITTY, I'VE BEEN TELLING HIM STORIES ABOUT YELLOW BEAR, A LITTLE KNIT BEAR HIS GRANDMA MADE.

I DECIDED NOW IS THE TIME TO COLLECT ALL THE BEDTIME STORIES INTO A BOOK. BUT... RANDOM HOUSE PASSED ON IT...

Sigh

TOP SHELF PASSED ON IT TOO.

TONIGHT, EVEN ELI PASSED ON IT.

No WAY, dude.

No.

Do you want a Yellow Bear story?

No, BATMAN STORY

OCTOBER 3, 2006

UMBRELLA FLOP

FLOP

Awww! My umbrella!

Actually, I like it better this way.

OCTOBER 4, 2006

MAGICAL REALISM

I really live some kind of charmed life.

What happened?

Well...in my strip the other day I mentioned that both Random House and Top Shelf passed on my Yellow Bear book...

...and someone from Chronicle Books saw that strip online and emailed me today to say THEY would be interested.

Nice

OCTOBER 5, 2006

BED TIME STORY

Eli wants you to tell him a story about Mommy and Daddy.

Okay!

And don't tell him a dirty one!

Geez! I won't

OCTOBER 6, 2006

SPECIAL MOMENTS

There's a funny patch of make-up smeared on your face.

I'll wipe it off... Hey!

DUCK

I guess this is going to be a fun date.

OCTOBER 7, 2006

BOYS & GIRLS

I'm going to be a man.

What's that?

Mens got short hair

OCTOBER 8, 2006

ELBOW CHEERS

Daddy! Cheers our elbows!

Cheers!

KLONK

STICK CHEATER

SNEAKING IN THE NEIGHBORS' WOODS FOR KINDLING

OCTOBER 9, 2006

STEP UP, SPANDY

Look, Spandy. I won a Harvey Award.

Wanna help me win another one?

OCTOBER 10, 2006

EMERGENCY

Wash your hands

Eee! Help! My fingers are drowning!

OCTOBER 11, 2006

DREAM WINDOW

ELI IS SLEEPING, TAKING HIS NAP...

BUT ONE EYE IS STILL OPEN.

I WAVE TO HIM THROUGH THE TINY BLACK WINDOW OF HIS EYEBALL.

Hi

MAYBE I CAN GET INTO HIS DREAM.

Hi sweetie

OCTOBER 12, 2006

*BACKWARDS SWIMMING

It's too bad backwards swimming isn't an Olympic sport.

I could be a gold medalist!

* SLOWLY

OCTOBER 13, 2006

A LITTLE JAMES?

He sounds just like a little James

Eli, are you a little James?

NO!

Ha! That sounds just like something James would say.

OCTOBER 14, 2006

DADDY WRATH

Eli!

what?

I said to stop stretching your shirt like that!!

why?

Because you're going to RUIN it! Now take it off!

I good! I good!

I won't stretch it anymore.

That's Right. Because I took it off you.

A "HAPPY SUNSHINE" STYLE
KOCHALKA QUALITY SHIRT

OCTOBER 15, 2006

CARTOON STUDIES

I'M GOING TO WHITE RIVER JUNCTION TODAY TO LECTURE ABOUT DOING DAILY DIARY COMIC STRIPS.

My ass is cold in this cold seat!

I'M GOING TO PENCIL THESE FIRST TWO PANELS ON THE BUS AND THEN FINISH THE STRIP & INK IT, LIVE IN FRONT OF THE CLASS.

Ah. Now my bottom's warming up.

I'm the tiniest bit drawing—

Uh—I'm the tiniest bit NERVOUS about drawing in FRONT of you

But I'll get over it.

How does your bottom feel?

OCTOBER 16, 2006

PROBABLY?

The doctor said the embryo isn't growing.

I'm probably going to miscarry

Oh honey... I'm so sorry I told everyone.

snif

I guess it doesn't matter... we don't love it that much yet...

...but we were going to love it so much

YESTERDAY

OCTOBER 17, 2006

DEAD OF NIGHT

I don't want to draw a diary strip anymore.

It hurts too much

It's embarrassing and stupid.

I'm retarded

THE NEXT DAY

That's kinda weird

A lot of new subscribers signed up for the strip today!

OCTOBER 18, 2006

ALL RIGHT IN THE CITY

I'M IN NEW YORK CITY

wheee

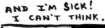
AND I'M SICK! I CAN'T THINK.

I WAS SURE TO PICK UP A COPY OF THE "NEW YORK PRESS" WHICH HAS AN INTERVIEW WITH ME. A GOOFY INTERVIEW ABOUT MAKING COMICS, AND MUSIC, AND BABIES.

I CAN'T LOOK AT THE AWFUL THING

OCTOBER 19, 2006

WAITING FOR GARY JAY

So... what's this Ryko guy look like?

Kinda like a heavy-metal elf.

XM

I DID AN INTERVIEW WITH XM SATELLITE RADIO AND SIGNED THIS CANVAS, NESTLED BETWEEN WHERE RICK SPRINGFIELD DREW A CARTOON OF HIS DOG AND A LITTLE SELF-PORTRAIT OF PHIL COLLINS

KOCHALKA

MTV JOE

NEW YORK CITY

OCTOBER 20, 2006

ROCK NIGHT

THERE WERE REAL BIG STARS IN THE AUDIENCE AND YOU CAN FUCKIN' BET THERE WAS A REAL BIG STAR UP ON THE STAGE. AND AS SICK AS I WAS, WHEN I GOT UP THERE IT EVAPORATED, DISPLACED BY ROCK POWER.

THEN AFTER THE SHOW AT THE MERCURY LOUNGE, SOME OF US TOOK A TAXI OVER TO A HONKY-TONK BAR CALLED 9C AND CROAKED OUT A FEW MORE SONGS

Sweet sweet CORN ON the cob

NEW YORK CITY

OCTOBER 21, 2006

GREAT EXPECTATIONS

I NEED TO SHAVE SO I CAN KISS MY FAMILY WHEN THEY GET HOME FROM GRANDMA'S

BUT INSTEAD I MOSTLY JUST FOUGHT WITH THEM

What are you doing?

FORGET it!

Nothing!

OCTOBER 22, 2006

You're a good husband

KISS

Do you want to come with me to the ultrasound appointment tomorrow?

I suppose I should.

Do you think they'll try to INDUCE right there?

No they'd probably schedule it for another time.

I need to get a haircut.

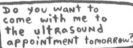

OCTOBER 23, 2006

PEANUT ULTRASOUND

Oh! It looks like a peanut.

Oh, wait! I saw a little face! It looks just like Eli! Oh my god!

As you can see there is a yolk sac but no fetal development at all.

oh

OCTOBER 24, 2006

THERE AND BACK AGAIN

Is it hard to be a rock star?

You've got to stay up late, get up early, and just keep Rocking!

OCTOBER 28, 2006

PLAYDATE

Want to know the best Part of being a Stay-at-home dad?

We had this play-date for the kids... All the moms were gorgeous and they kept popping their tits out!

OCTOBER 29, 2006

GIG MONEY

Here ya go Creston.

So, everyone got a different amount.

I based it on a complicated algorhythm and a system of merits and demerits

How do you get demerits?

If you fuckin annoy me.

OCTOBER 30, 2006

COSTUMED

SPOON!

YOUR muscles ARE SO FAT!

Amy... do you want me to carry your back-pack so your cape looks better?

No, it's okay

She's a HUNCHBACK SUPER HERO!

Yeah

OCTOBER 31, 2006

SWEETIE THE MOTH

Sweetie!

No!

Go back outside

Oh! she flew into the light.

Sweetheart! Come down from there!!

Sweetie!

NOVEMBER 1, 2006

CHOOSE YOUR PATH TO ADVENTURE

Do you want to go swimming?

No...

Not today

Should we get haircuts?

Yes!

NOVEMBER 1, 2006

LETTER TO DECLAN

This is a tunnel with monsters. They have BLOOD POWERS coming out.

Okay, put it in the envelope.

Declan's gonna be SO scared!

NOVEMBER 2, 2006

SOUNDSCAN SUPERSTAR

I GOT THE SOUNDSCAN REPORTS FOR "SPREAD YOUR EVIL WINGS AND FLY" TODAY

CLICK

We've only sold 177 copies! The label probably invested $10,000 in that album

I'll be dropped for sure

hunh

NOVEMBER 3, 2006

THREE PILLS

Three pills in your vagina ♪♫

Hey! Don't be mean.

I'm being nice. I wrote a song.

NOVEMBER 3, 2006

BITTERSWEETHEART

I guess I feel a little sad, but I also feel relieved.

I feel sad and kind of giddy

NOVEMBER 4, 2006

SUN AND MOON

It's dark!

Yup, it got dark while we were in the movie.

Are you surprised?

Yes

Hey, maybe the sun and moon are playing a game.

When the moon comes out the sun hides and then when the sun comes out the moon runs and hides

LAST NIGHT

NOVEMBER 5, 2006

A FRESH START

AMY STAYED HOME FROM WORK AND WE SPENT THE DAY CLEANING THE HOUSE. IT SUCKED.

Stop arguing with me!

I'm not arguing, it's just impossible to know what's going to make you mad

Yes you are!

Stop being such a jerk!

Admit you're arguing with me!

NOVEMBER 6, 2006

CATS DON'T VOTE

Spandy, did you vote today?

Yawn

You did?

STRETCH

Good! Then you can have a sticker.

I VOTED

NOVEMBER 7, 2006

ONCE UPON A TIE

You looked up how to tie a tie online?

Yeah

AT THE PARTY

I tied it myself

NOVEMBER 8, 2006

THE CONUNDRUM

Are you coming to the store with me after dinner?

I don't know

I should stay home to draw my comic strip. But if I go with you to the store maybe something interesting will happen that I could draw my strip about.

That's the CONUNDRUM you face each day. Live the life that will make your art more interesting, OR work on your art.

NOVEMBER 9, 2006

LOOK OUT, IT'S JAMMY TIME

Your jammies have flowers?

I like flowers

I like flowers and sparkles.

Everyone likes flowers and sparkles.

Everyone except the Anti Flower-Sparkle League.

NOVEMBER 10, 2006

LASER WOLF

WE WENT TO SEE FIDDLER ON THE ROOF

Where's the fiddler on the roof??

He's not in every scene

She's going to marry Laser Wolf.

LASER WOLF!?

Did they really say "Laser Wolf"? That would be such an awesome name for a superhero, or something.

Where's the fiddler on the roof

INTERMISSION

I'll carry Eli home and you and Grandma can stay and watch the rest.

Really?

Yawn

NOVEMBER 11, 2006

CHIMNEY KOCHALKA

What's that?

This? It's the chimney for the wood stove.

And the smoke goes out out up the chimney by the window at your bedroom?

That's Right

My bedroom doesn't have one by my window.

Don't worry

...you can share mine with me.

Oh, good!

NOVEMBER 12, 2006

THE NOVELIST

IT'S NATIONAL NOVEL-WRITING MONTH OR SOMETHING, SO I'VE BEEN WORKING ON MY YELLOW BEAR NOVEL.

It's so fuckin' good!

BUT AMY SAYS THAT IF IT'S FOR CHILDREN AND ONLY 16 PAGES LONG, THEN IT'S NOT A NOVEL.

Why do you call it a novel?

It's not a novel

Well it's got chapters.

And when I add pictures it will be a little bit longer

Why not just call it a children's book?

Can I call it a "bedtime novel"?

NOVEMBER 13, 2006

ALL BUSINESS

COLIN CAME OVER TO PRACTICE FOR OUR SHOW

How are you doing?

You already asked and I already told you

No I didn't.

Yeah

When you first came in you said "How are you doing" and I said "good."

But really I'm not so good.

The phone has NO dialtone

And the internet doesn't work

SOON

FLOOSHH

Well, your toilet works

NOVEMBER 14, 2006

NO DIAL TONE, NO INTERNET

I'M ALIVE

What's this funny feeling I have?

Maybe it's 'cause there's nothing to jerk off to?

NOVEMBER 15, 2006

ROCKET BALLOONS $1.99 PER BAG

EEEEEE

NOVEMBER 16, 2006

FEELING SQUEEMISHY

WHILE CARRYING ONE OF ELI'S LITTLE FRIENDS*

Uh, Finny... stop pinching your bellybutton

Put your hands in your pockets

Could you maybe wait to do that in private

*(YESTERDAY)

NOVEMBER 17, 2006

PRETTY LITTLE BUG

Some little bugs go to school. Some little bugs go to work. Some little bugs stay home, And blow their nose on their shirt!

Some little bugs eat toothpaste. Some little bugs drink pee. Some little bugs are ugly...

~but you're a PRETTY little bug to me!

Say it THREE more times!

NOVEMBER 18, 2006

Wii WILL DESTROY YOU

why no Nintendo the Wii?

They're sold out

39

3

Everyone got here earlier and got vouchers... special tickets. We don't have a ticket so we can't get a Wii

SORRY honey

Let's knock 'em down and have a GIANT BATTLE!

NOVEMBER 19, 2006

INTO THE LIGHT

I WANT SOME DAZZLE OUT OF LIFE

I WANT SOME COMIC BOOK OR VIDEO GAME TO MELT THE WORLD

I WANT TO STARE INTO THE LIGHT

TO LOVE AND LIVE AND DIE WITHOUT BLINKING

BLINK BLINK BLINK

NOVEMBER 20, 2006

THIS MORNING, I SHAVED.

LAST NIGHT, I HAD A DREAM ABOUT SHAVING MY FACE THAT WAS SORT OF LIKE A SERIES OF NEW YORKER SINGLE-PANEL CARTOONS BUT DRAWN IN THE STYLE OF THE LITTLE LULU COMIC BOOKS.

"THIS IS WHAT I WAS TRYING TO AVOID."

NOVEMBER 21, 2006

TELEPORTATION

You've yelled at me ENOUGH today

If you want to yell at me any more you have to wait till tomorrow.

That's so mean!

What? I think that's fair

NOVEMBER 22, 2006

THANKSGIVING

Slash

Slice

Swoosh

SOON I'm killing everyone in the whole family except you and me and mommy.

NOVEMBER 23, 2006

I DROP THE TURKEY BOMB

Well, I pooped out a whole turkey.

No... you didn't.

NOVEMBER 24, 2006

ZYGHOST

THE GHOST OF OUR DEAD ZYGOTE

what do you want? Leave me alone.

The baby monster is following us.

!!!

NOVEMBER 25, 2006

READING STUFF

"You don't Read my books, do you?"
"SuRe I do"

"I haven't Read any of those "Reinventing" things or super-effers... But I think I Read the first Sketchbook diaries"

"Geez, that was YEARS ago..." (2001)

"But Still she loves me."
!?

NOVEMBER 26, 2006

ELI'S CHRISTMAS TREE

"It's fun to draw stuff."

"Spandy's pine-needle vomit"

NOVEMBER 27, 2006

BREATHE DEEP

"James! I came back"
"Let me give you a BIG HUG!"

"mmm..."
"You smell like PRE SCHOOL!"

NOVEMBER 27, 2006

INVISIBLE RAIN

"I FORGOT MY HAT AND GLOVES AT MY PARENT'S HOUSE SO MY MOM MAILED THEM TO ME."

"THEY WERE SEVERAL TIMES BIGGER THAN THE BOX THEY CAME IN"

NOW I'VE GOT SOMETHING TO WEAR IN THE COLD

"bRAr"
"invisible Rain"

NOVEMBER 28, 2006

ADULT SUPERVISION

Amy! Your ass is cold

Yeah, I suffer from Cold Ass Syndrome.

C.A.S.

Eli's downstairs

He's totally unsupervised without supervision.

NOVEMBER 29, 2006

DOODLE PIDDLE

WHILE TRYING TO DECIDE WHAT TO DRAW, I DREW THIS DOODLE

THEN I DREW ANOTHER

BECAUSE OF THE WAY ELI'S FORESKIN IS SHAPED, HIS PEE TENDS TO SQUIRT STRAIGHT UP, SO SOMETIMES IF HE'S SITTING ON THE TOILET IT WILL SQUIRT UP UNDER THE TOILET SEAT...

Oh. Whoops.

Eli...

Push your penis down more

NOVEMBER 30, 2006

GEEK SEEKER

So, I was at this website ps3seeker.com/wii

and they claim your store will have the Wii for sale on Sunday.

But you don't get shipments on Sundays, do you?

No... for them to be HERE ON Sunday, we would've had to gotten 'em today. And if they came in today I'd sell you one RIGHT NOW.

Heh. That's what I thought

DECEMBER 1, 2006

THIS ACTUALLY HAPPENED ON THANKSGIVING, BUT WHEN I TOLD THE STORY TO MY NEIGHBOR HE SUGGESTED THAT IT'S NOT TOO LATE TO DRAW

THE DEAD SQUIRREL STORY

HERE'S a stick to poke the squirrel with

He's got beautiful fur.

AND THERE'S HIS PENIS

flip

Now I'll flip him back again.

Flip him back OVER so we CAN see his PENIS again.

DECEMBER 2, 2006

Wii SO CRAZY

I COULD BARELY SLEEP LAST NIGHT. THE MOON WAS SO BRIGHT.

I WOKE UP A DOZEN TIMES, READY TO SPRING INTO ACTION FIRST THING IN THE MORNING. GOT TO CIRCUIT CITY AS THE SUN WAS COMING UP.

I'VE GOT THE BEST SPOT IN LINE

with my friend the tree

THREE HOURS LATER WE HEAD HOME WITH OUR NINTENDO Wii, IN A CONSUMERIST HIGH!

I had SO much FUN waiting in line.

Wii

Wii BOXING FULFILLS ELI'S EVERY 3-YEAR-OLD FANTASY:

I'm SO STRONG!

POW

DECEMBER 3, 2006

ENTER THE HYPNOVERSE

YOUR eyelids are heavy & happy. You can't keep them open. YOUR eyelids are falling asleep.

YOUR eyelids are heavy and happy. You can't keep them open. YOUR eyelids are falling asleep.

ARE you asleep?

DECEMBER 4, 2006

A MOMENT OF FOLLY

Is her tummy getting fatter?

what's WRONG?

Uh... I can't say.

What? what did you do?

James.

I didn't do anything and NOTHING'S WRONG.

You're upset

what's WRONG?

You can tell me, I'll help you.

I SWEAR Nothing is WRONG

DECEMBER 5, 2006

NIGHT VISITOR

SPANDY JUMPS UP ON THE BED.

AT LEAST I THINK IT'S HER. MY EYES ARE CLOSED AND I'M FALLING ASLEEP.

DECEMBER 6, 2006

DREAM CAR

I DREAMT THE CAR WAS MADE OUT OF WOOD AND IT WAS ALL ROTTED OUT AROUND THE WINDOWS

DECEMBER 6, 2006

THE HUMAN HEAD

Eli was playing with her today and doing somersaults ...so their heads were in the same place.

We should check for head lice.

Hmm... that could be a nit. Or maybe a booger.

DECEMBER 7, 2006

BEAUTIFUL WORLD

I WAS ON THE PHONE WHEN SUDDENLY A GLINTING SPARKLE CAUGHT MY EYE.

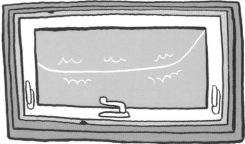

IS that a CRACK in OUR BRAND NEW WINDOW

DECEMBER 8, 2006

SET UP

SETTING UP MY NEW COMPUTER... SEVEN HOURS (& COUNTING) TO TRANSFER FILES FROM THE OLD ONE.

Go! Go!

TRANSFERING INFORMATION

DIDN'T HAVE A TANTRUM SETTING UP THE CHRISTMAS TREE THIS YEAR, BECAUSE THIS YEAR I LET AMY DO IT.

I think me & Eli are allergic to the tree.

Snif

me too, Snif

ha-choo!

DECEMBER 9, 2006

INVISIBLE SPACESHIP

MADE FROM A wii CONTROLLER'S PACKAGING

CUT

And you can put your little guy in through the back and he can use it as a spaceship.

ZOOM

DECEMBER 10, 2006

NEW ARRANGEMENT

LIVING ROOM BEFORE THE CHRISTMAS TREE:

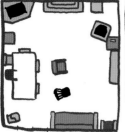

LIVING ROOM WITH THE CHRISTMAS TREE:

A GOUGE ON THE WALL FROM WHERE THE COUCH USED TO BE (CLOSE UP):

DECEMBER 11, 2006

LULLABY

I'll tuck you in & punch your nose,

Karate chop, ♪ ♪

—and tickle your toes ♪

—until you fall asleep! Until you fall asleep... ♪

DECEMBER 12, 2006

FIVE CHOPSTICKS

look! Five chopsticks

I'll be able to pick up a lot of sushi this way, won't I?

It's too bad we didn't bring Spandy. I bet Spandy would like sushi. Kitties love fish.

Wow! The college girl at the other table has a GORGEOUS little body!

Spandy doesn't know what fish are.

DECEMBER 13, 2006

THE BLANK PAGE

AS I STARE AT MY SKETCHBOOK, TRYING TO DECIDE WHAT TO DRAW TODAY, IT STARTS FLASHING COLORS AT ME.

RED

BLUE

YELLOW

Am I about to pass out?

~~AUGUST~~ 14, 2006
DECEMBER

TWO BAD KNIGHTS

I love the PRINCESS

I love the PRINCESS even though I'm a BAD KNIGHT

I love the PRINCESS too!

Nice bra & panties!

DECEMBER 15, 2006

TOGETHERNESS

WATCHING VERONICA MARS ON DVD

Amy! You're asleep.

I'm trying to stay awake.

No you're not.

If you were trying to stay awake you'd SIT UP instead of lying down.

Oh, forget it. You can sleep if you want, I'm sure you need it.

DECEMBER 16, 2006

FOREST DEFENDERS

ME, TURNER, DECLAN, ELI AND FINN

EVIL!

WACK

THUMP

DECEMBER 17, 2006

CONGRATULATIONS

MY SONG* WAS NAMED ONE OF THE TOP 100 SONGS OF THE YEAR BY ROLLING STONE

BRITNEY's on the dance floor wearing silver pants

What a delightful song to sing

RING

Thanks! It's pretty cool. I wonder if BRITNEY's heard the song yet?

Maybe she'll SUE me

* BRITNEY'S SILVER CAN

DECEMBER 18, 2006

SNOW AWESOME

PICKING ELI UP FROM PRESCHOOL:

he's gonna LOVE this!

5 MINUTES LATER...

DECEMBER 19, 2006

JINGLE CATS

A COUPLE DOZEN OR MORE OF US WENT CAROLING

Silent Night... ♪

Holy Night... ♪

I'm in Rolling Stone

I ALSO WROTE AN ORIGINAL CHRISTMAS SONG JUST FOR US ALL TO SING TONIGHT

Jingle cat, Jingle cat, Jingle Cat, Meow! ♪♪

WOW!

DECEMBER 20, 2006

BAD ENOUGH

Amy has the day off from work tomorrow...

But Eli's in PRE school

That means you can have Sex in the daylight!

If you REALLY want to know when we have sex, I could just send you an email every time we do it.

No! YOUR strip is bad ENOUGH!

DECEMBER 21, 2006

SEXMAS

I might not be done my Christmas shopping...

I still haven't got you anything SEXY yet.

oh

Christmas is NOT sexy.

DECEMBER 22, 2006

CHRISTMAS IS COMING

Spandy, should I change your litter box...

OR should I wait to see if Santa does it?

DECEMBER 23, 2006

SUPERSTARDOM

MY NEICE PAIGE JUST FIGURED OUT THAT I'M KINDA FAMOUS...

I can't believe I can actually TOUCH you.

Touch. Touch. Touch. Touch.

I can touch you too.

You should take him to school and charge the kids a nickle to touch him.

DECEMBER 24, 2006

CHICKEN WITH PLUMS BY MARJANE SATRAPI

HAT

MAGNETICALLY POWERED FLASHLIGHT

GLOVES

UMBRELLA *

SWEATER

PRINCESS MONONOKE DVD

CANDY HATS *

IN THE STUDIO

TWO PAIRS OF PANTS

ELEBITS FOR NINTENDO Wii

3 PAIRS OF SOCKS

DECEMBER 25, 2006

* (THESE TWO FROM ELI)

BOTTOM PINCHERS

I'd like to RUN with you...

But I'm afraid the lobsters in my backpack would get dizzy

-And they might pinch your bottom.

DECEMBER 26, 2006

FRONT SEAT BACK SEAT

ELI & I NOW BOTH HAVE WINTER HATS KNITTED BY MARIPOSA'S GRANDPA. IN THIS SCENE WE'RE DRIVING HOME FROM CHARLOTTE'S WEB!

Eli?

what?

I love you.

Daddy?

what?

Nothing!

MOCK SURPRISE

DECEMBER 27, 2006

GRAPEFRUIT PEEL CANDY

Go BACK to BED!

Wait... do you have to use the potty?

yes

I was playing with my dream friends. A girl was sharing her toys with me, but I couldn't see her

I'm making candy. It will be ready in the morning.

BLOOP

DECEMBER 28, 2006

THE END OF DAYS

Burning cat puke in the woodstove. It's a small pleasure.

TOSS

DECEMBER 29, 2006

SLED ATTACK

Attack!

MARIPOSA

LATER

What a great vacation! We consumed so much WINE, had so much SEX, and I played so many video games

And it FINALLY snowed.

DECEMBER 30, 2006

SPANKIN' DEMO

And Eli was naked and he was drumming on his tummy and his bottom at the same time, like this.

SPANK

THUMP

Ooh! Very nice. Do that again.

Um. Forget it.

↑ AMY'S OLD COLLEGE FRIENDS

DECEMBER 31, 2006

HAPPY NEW YEAR

AT MIDNIGHT I WAS COLORING MY STRIP & GETTING READY TO POST IT.

AMY CAME DOWNSTAIRS & TOLD ME TO HURRY UP.

I CHECKED THE CLOCK WIDGET ON MY COMPUTER

NEW YORK

AND WE KISSED AT PRECISELY TWO SECONDS AFTER MIDNIGHT.

JANUARY 1, 2007

THE ARGUMENT

Taruko paloochi gazee gah zo!

Taruko PALOOCHI CRICKA NUTCH!

LATER, AT NAP TIME:

We had a terrible argument, didn't we?

Yes

Karoochi kochalka kachinga.

We can teach mommy our Kochalka language when she gets home.

JANUARY 2, 2007

BABY TEETH

Sometimes, when people lose their baby teeth, they like to put them under their pillow.

Do you know why?

Yes

why?

Because they DON'T LIKE baby teeth!

JANUARY 3, 2007

FURTHER ADVENTURES OF YELLOW BEAR

A letter from Chronicle Books. It couldn't be a contract, could it?

Oh. They returned my Yellow Bear manuscript. It's a rejection letter.

What's this other package? Nintendo. Must be the Wii Replacement straps.

Neato!

Everything evens out. I'm happy!

Come on, Eli

JANUARY 4, 2007

MESSAGE TO THE PEOPLE

SHOUTED FROM THE BALCONY IN THE CHILDREN'S LIBRARY:

PEOPLE!

WAR is REAL and it KILLS PEOPLE!

JANUARY 4, 2006

DREAM GOOD

You know how sometimes you have a dream that's SO good...

...and you wake up just feeling good!

I had a dream like that last night.

I dreamt that me & Josh were making fun of NEW GUY!

JANUARY 5, 2006

POPEYE K.O.

WHENEVER THE STORY STARTS TO GET REALLY EXCITING IN POPEYE...

JUST WHEN I'M REALLY STARTING TO GET INTO IT...

I FALL ASLEEP.

Z

JANUARY 6, 2006

GENERAL POLICY

Josh, I had this dream that I saw a black & white still photograph of you naked. You were tan all over except a pale white patch at your pubic area because you had shaved after you tanned.

Anyhow, it's my general policy to tell people any dreams I have about them.

That's your "general policy"?

JANUARY 7, 2006

CHILDREN OF MEN

WALKING FROM THE CAR TO THE MOVIE THEATRE JASON EXTENDS HIS HAND

AND I TAKE HIS HAND IN MINE

JUST BRIEFLY BEFORE LETTING GO.

Weee!

JANUARY 8, 2006

I FEEL RICH

WHEN I BOUGHT MY Wii I FELT NO REMORSE.

WHEN I BOUGHT MY NEW iMAC, ABOUT A WEEK LATER, I FELT NO REMORSE.

WHEN I BOUGHT MY HIGH-DEF LCD TV LAST WEEK I FELT FINE. THEN WHILE SETTING IT UP I WAS HIT WITH A TIDAL WAVE OF CRUSHING REMORSE, MY HEART BURST THROUGH MY CHEST AND I WENT BLIND, INSANE.

BUT THEN I GOT OVER IT.   JANUARY 9, 2006

SNOW DAY

ehn neh

when the stick went in my eye, did I cry? No.

Did I whimper?

Yes

Were you worried?

Yes, I thought you were going to die.

JANUARY 10, 2007

PRINTER'S PROOFS

FOR AMERICAN ELF BOOK TWO

I wonder how much these are worth... $300?

FEDEX

What is it?

Printer's proof. They're just paper.

SHAKE

FEDEX

Is the paper worth $300? You can only insure it for the value of the paper itself.

That's ridiculous. It cost $300 to make it.

Look, imagine it was a check. You couldn't insure a check for $300.

That's totally different!

You don't understand! YOU don't understand! Look, if it gets destroyed and a claim is filed it's not going to be between me & YOU, so there's no need for US to argue.

SORRY

JANUARY 11, 2007

MY COMIC STRIP

While watching Metropolis Eli reached to grab my hair and poked me in the eye.

I thought maybe he scratched my cornea... but I guess not.

That was Wednesday, right? I got poked in the eye by a stick the same day!

You didn't mention it

Well, I wrote about it in my strip.

I don't read that Smutty thing.

JANUARY 12, 2006

GIRL'S NIGHT OUT

I'm going out with Josh now. You should wake Eli up in an hour & have dinner.

And we'll make love when you get home?

You can order out or you can make ham sandwiches.

You'll be okay, right?

I guess if I get too horny, I can always jerk myself off...

Onto your ham sandwich?

JANUARY 13, 2007

IN

And we'll put the food inside my coat and sneak it into the theater.

So

We're sneaking in!

& OUT

Thanks for picking us up Dave.*

We locked the keys in the car but everything turned out FINE. Mommy didn't cry and Daddy didn't yell at anyone.

I got disappointed

* AMY'S BROTHER

JANUARY 14, 2007

FRIENDS OF MAGIC

YESTERDAY WE MADE MONSTER TREATS

Gravel & Snow mixed together

It's a sweet dessert for monsters.

I can smash it?

DON'T smash it!

TODAY WE MADE PARTY HOUSES FOR ICE FAIRIES

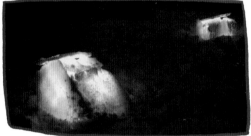

JANUARY 15, 2007

BE CAREFUL!

Come on, Eli! Don't stand on the handles

I'm being careful.

Yeah, but I'M NOT!

PUSH

Sorry!

"Yeah, but I'm Not!" BOOM!

Do it do it again!

JANUARY 16, 2007

PORCH CHAIR

What's our chair doing in the SNOWbank?

How'd it get there?

Teenagers?

Yeah, TEENAGERS

JANUARY 17, 2007

ICE LESSONS

CHANK

Oh no!

I forgot to tell you... if you drop an icicle, it breaks.

Aw

JANUARY 18, 2007

SECRET SUPERMAN

!!!

I already own that issue of Superman, don't I?

Yeah. I bought it and then forgot about it. I wonder where I put it? It must be lost in the house somewhere...

I should go home and look for it.

Or maybe it would be easier just to buy another copy right now.

I don't know!

JANUARY 19, 2007

SENSE SENSATION

SNOW BLOWS OFF THE ROOF OF THE CHINESE RESTAURANT AS THE SUN BREAKS THROUGH THE CLOUDS.

Sunshine & snow in my face and the smell of HOT OIL!

JANUARY 20, 2007

GOING ON A MOVIEDATE WITH MY LOVELY WIFE

PAN'S LABYRINTH

Hold my hand.

Should we have another baby?

Why not?

Well...

If I never see another movie where someone's face gets smashed in with a bottle, I'll be happy.

JANUARY 21, 2007

SO INTENSE

I'M TRYING TO COMPLETE 150 NEW PAINTINGS FOR MY SHOW AT GIANT ROBOT IN NYC.

AND I'M TRYING TO MAKE THEM ALL AS AWESOME AS POSSIBLE.

Must prove to the world that I'm a GREAT PAINTER!

Ah!... CRAMP!

How did I cramp my FOOT?!

JANUARY 22, 2007

WINTER WARMTH

NICE HOT COFFEE AND A NICE HOT SHOWER

Warm, inside & out

PAINTER'S PROGRESS

dragged my sleve in the paint

LATER I did it AGAIN!

ehn!

JANUARY 23, 2007

TOO MANY WHYS

"So, Zuzu went to the boy's house"

Why?

The book doesn't say WHY the book merely states that it happened!

JANUARY 24, 2007

OH THE SNOWMANITY

OUR SNOWMAN SLUMPED OVER & HIS EYES FELL OUT

It looks like he's bending over to pick them up.

Hey!

KRAK

JANUARY 25, 2007

TIC-TAC-TOE

BY ELI & JAMES KOCHALKA

ELI AND DADDY WERE PLAYING TIC-TAC-TOE ON A PIECE OF PAPER.

DADDY DREW AN X

AND ELI CRIED BECAUSE HE DIDN'T WANT THE X TO BE THERE.

I don't want to play anymore

Do you want to draw a comic about playing Tic-Tac-Toe?

No!

JANUARY 26, 2007

THE END.

UNIVERSAL LOVE

JANUARY 27, 2007

SQUEAKY HULK

WE LIKE TO PLAY THAT THE HULK TALKS IN A VERY HIGH-PITCHED VOICE:

JANUARY 28, 2007

SUCKY TREAT

JANUARY 29, 2007

WINTER MOSQUITTO

JANUARY 30, 2007

SHARK WEAPON

Sand Boy has a weapon shaped like a shark.

Sand Boy is spelled E-l-i

I can make that shark weapon for you out of cardboard

Would you like that?

SOON

JANUARY 31, 2007

TAX GLITCH

LAST YEAR, VERMONT SCREWED UP AND ACCIDENTALLY APPLIED MY FIRST "ESTIMATED-TAX" PAYMENT OF THE 2006 TAX YEAR TO MY 2005 TAXES, AND THEN CUT ME A REFUND CHECK FOR IT. WHEN I POINTED OUT THEIR MISTAKE & AFTER MUCH WRANGLING, I GOT THEM TO TAKE THE CHECK BACK AND APPLY IT TO MY 2006 TAXES LIKE THEY WERE ORIGINALLY SUPPOSED TO. BUT NOW THEY'VE SENT ME A 1099-G FOR THAT AMOUNT, MEANING I'M SUPPOSED TO DECLARE THIS AS INCOME & ACTUALLY PAY TAX ON IT!

Yes, that's right.

Because it was brought forward from your 2005 taxes

But they were NEVER supposed to apply it to my 2005 tax in the first place!

No, they told me it was a computer glitch!

FEBRUARY 1, 2007

THE JOY OF SEX & LOVE

YESTERDAY, UPSTAIRS IN THE LIBRARY

So, we're pretty much trying to have another baby...

PP

Mostly just to make the sex more fun.

But you've made the decision? Good!

I think it's the best possible reason to have a baby.

Sex?

Yeah

FEBRUARY 2, 2007

ANIMAL TRACKERS

TRACKING LITTLE ANIMALS THROUGH THE WOODS

BRANCHES SNAPPING OFF AROUND US AS WE SQUEEZE THROUGH TIGHT PLACES.

SNAP

SNAP

SNAP

THE CREATURE STOPPED TO CHECK OUT EACH OF THESE GAS HATCHES THAT ARE IN THE WOODS.

FEBRUARY 3, 2007

E COMB

"James, look"

"It's an E with too many lines."

"Is that what Eli said?"

"Yes"

"Well, he's right! That E has way too many lines."

FEBRUARY 4, 2007

MAILMAN ON THE PORCH

FOOTSTEPS THUMP THUMP MAILBOX CLANK

"The mailman came early today."

THUMP THUMP

LATER

"There's no mail"

"Hey! Then who was on my porch?!"

FEBRUARY 5, 2007

THE CRUST

POCH

"That's the thickest crust I've ever seen on snow!"

"I'm bringing some home"

FEBRUARY 6, 2007

HELLO!

"Top Shelf sent me a magazine from England that reviewed one of my comics but it was a PORN MAGAZINE."

"I almost pulled it out of the envelope in front of everyone in the post office. It was embarrassing"

"Then you RAN HOME as fast as you could?"

"No, it was gross. It had gross old moms in it & stuff."

"Like 37 year-olds?"

37

"Honey! Splayed out in BRIGHT LIGHT"

FEBRUARY 7, 2007

SPANDY'S CHAIR

SPANDY NOW HAS HER OWN CHAIR THAT'S EXACTLY JUST HER SIZE.

Oh my God. That's just too cute.

I kinda feel bad about saying she's not such a great cat in that interview I did.

I mean... she throws up a lot and she hates Eli... but look at her on that chair!

FEBRUARY 8, 2007

FATHERLY WATER

SLURP

Does water taste better from Daddy's hand?
Yup

Really?
Yeah

FEBRUARY 9, 2007

ELI'S HAIRCUT

Hey, that boy has Eli's old haircut.

He must've grabbed your hair off the floor of The Hairy Bear * and glued it to his head.

* KID'S BARBERSHOP   FEBRUARY 10, 2007

YELLOW BLOBS

Oh!

When I first saw those yellow blobs I thought they were Lisa and Homer Simpson.

FEBRUARY 11, 2007

TRYING

We need to buy a new kitten, for the Monster Puncher book I'm working on.

Okay.

Or maybe we should just try to make one.

You mean instead of a human baby..?

Can we do that?

Well, we can try.

And it would be a lot less responsibility & less expensive ...shorter lifespan...

FEBRUARY 12, 2007

GLOBAL WARMING COMICS

Ouch

That's classic cold!

FEBRUARY 13, 2007

~ VALENTINE'S DAY BLIZZARD ~
LOVE IS BLIND

my eyes are filling up with SNOW!

STATE OF THE UNION

It's always such a surprise when people break up.

Couples should really give yearly "State of the Union" addresses to their friends

FEBRUARY 14, 2007

DISASTER DAY

why isn't the furnace working?

OH YEAH! I FORGOT THAT IT AUTOMATICALLY SHUTS OFF IF THE EXHAUST VENT IS BLOCKED.*

POP

ME & ELI GO SWIMMING IN THE SNOW

Ha! ha!

* WHICH SAVED OUR LIVES!

FEBRUARY 15, 2007

WALKING IN THE STREET, SIDEWALKS PLUGGED WITH SNOW

NO SIDEWALKS

NEW HAIRCUT UNDER HAT

RUMBLE

I hope my body doesn't get crushed before I can make it to my big art opening in NYC...

STILL, I CAN'T BE BOTHERED TO GET OUT OF THE WAY

FEBRUARY 16, 2007

BEAUTIFUL
OCTOPUS

PHOEBE CATES AT MY ART OPENING

My wife loved your single.

?? YOUR SEVEN-inch

It was her favorite song that year

Is she retarded?

LATER, BACK STAGE, AT MY ROCK SHOW

When Phoebe Cates talks, her philtrum quivers.

her filtrum?

Right here

It pinches in & out like the mouth of a squid or an octopus

NYC

FEBRUARY 17, 2007

RED DOTS

I Sold 48 paintings tonight!

I love Red dots!

GIANT ROBOT & CAKE-SHOP, NYC

FEBRUARY 18, 2007

MOMMA'S BABY

Momma was going to have a baby & it was growing bigger an' bigger-

And then it POPPED!!

it was sooo funny

Actually, momma was pretty sad.

Nope. funny

FEBRUARY 19, 2007

TWILIGHT PRINCESS

ELI WAS SENT HOME EARLY FROM PRESCHOOL FOR BEING SICK, SO INSTEAD OF DOING MY TAXES...

...we defeated Ganondorf!

Look at Midna! She's beautiful

LATER:

Do you think it's funny that I teared up at the end of Legend of Zelda?

Yes, but I bet that online you could find lots of people who did.

FEBRUARY 20, 2007

CITY CHICKENS

FLAP
FLAP
FLAP

They can fly! Make it fly again!

IDOLINE

I wrote a song about you.

Oh?!

Yeah, but I forgot it.

FEBRUARY 21, 2007

THE PRINCESS' ROBOT

We've got to uncover the princess's Robot!

No! That's not her Robot! It's evil! He captured the Princess!

What!?

Tell us where the Princess is!

KLONK

FEBRUARY 22, 2007

THRILLING

MY HEART WAS POUNDING THE WHOLE TIME I DID MY TAXES

I WANTED TO RUN AWAY AND DRAW ICICLES, BUT WAS CAUGHT IN THE GRIP OF THE VORTEX.

FEB 23, 2007

FEBRUARY 24, 2007

MY DINNER WITH JELLO

JELLO BIAFRA WAS LATE SO WE WERE FINISHED EATING BY THE TIME HE GOT THERE

Get any good records?

Ug. Maybe I shouldn't have pulled this tape off

Do you want it?

Sure.

Gee, that's real nice tape.

FEBRUARY 24, 2007

GOOD HUMOUR

That's too big and a half!

Ha ha! That's funny.

No it's NOT!

FEBRUARY 25, 2007

HOW TO CHASE A CAT
WITHOUT EVEN TRYING

Spandy! why are you running? No one is chasing the cat.

Everything's not all about you.

LATER Phoo! I "almost caught her."

FEBRUARY 26, 2007

RED SPOTS

Oh, poor sweetie ...you've got so many little red spots on you

You're the one that wanted to make love in the bright daylight.

I'm sorry!

FEBRUARY 27, 2007

FLOPPY

I still think this might be a women's sweater

But I rock it

Right?

FEBRUARY 28, 2007

UP ON THE ROOF

??

I'm shutting the window

Eli, don't shut the window

Eli! Don't Shut the Window!

I don't want to see you die.

MARCH 1, 2007

ROLLING SPIT

SNOW STICKS TO THE SPIT AS IT ROLLS DOWN, BECOMING A FLUFFY BLOBBY BALL.

SPUT

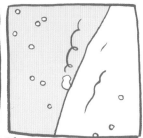

CLIMBING BACK UP

I can't climb up.

Follow me

I'll make a ladder of foot-prints

Ow!

NORTH SPRINGFIELD, VT

MARCH 2, 2007

SNOW FRUIT

ADVENTURE IN THE WOODS AT TWILIGHT

MARCH 3, 2007

LITTLE BED

Once upon a time, yellow Bear fell asleep.

The end.

ha ha ha hee hee

Ha ha ha hee hee hee

MARCH 4, 2007

FATHER'S MIND

Hi, this is James.

Ahhh! James, James...

J-A-M-E-S, James. I know you, right?

I'm your son. James.

MARCH 5, 2007

VOTE TOGETHER

Shall we go vote now? We NEVER get to vote together!

Yeah

Do you want to hold my penis while we do it?

No.

MARCH 6, 2007

JOYS AND DISAPPOINTMENTS MARCH 7, 2007

SPANDY'S NEW FAVORITE CHAIR IS ELI'S BEAR CHAIR.

THERE WAS A REALLY AMAZING WEIRD ICICLE HANGING FROM THE FURNACE VENT BUT IT BROKE OFF.

SUPERMAN AND BIZARRO SUPERMAN USE A GIANT SCISSOR TO OPEN A PACKAGE FROM AMAZON.COM.

A LITTLE BIT GRUMPY IN THE EVENING.

Nothing!

MARCH 7, 2007

KNUCKLES

My knuckles itch.

Scritch scritch scritch

The more I scratch them against my whiskers, the more they itch.

In other news, Amy's pregnant again.

(But it's too early to mention)

MARCH 8, 2007

BIG DUMB VISITOR

Doggy, we're not your people

This not your house

Oh fine.

??

Hisss!

Rarf!?

MARCH 9, 2007

HUMMUS LUNCH

POP

BABY

My sandwich came back to life!

MARCH 10, 2007

BIG MELT

LAST NIGHT ALL THE SNOW STARTED MELTING AND IT DRIPPED THROUGH THE WALLS OF THE BASEMENT SO I HAD TO MOVE MY BOXES OF COMICS & CDS AROUND.

Cat pee?

No...

THIS MORNING WE WOKE UP TO A STRONG SMELL OF SKUNK IN THE HOUSE WHICH SEEMED TO BE COMING FROM THE BASEMENT, BUT...

phug!

I think maybe a skunk died under our porch or something and then when the snow melted, the water brought the stink with it down into the basement?

MARCH 11, 2007

STAPLER PANIC

Amy, I can't find my stapler!

Where could it be?!

Did I leave it at the post office?

I can take you to get one tomorrow

But I need it RIGHT NOW!

And I was SO careful not to lose it. I don't WANT to buy a new one.

Why not?

AMY, THE SWEETEST GIRL IN THE WORLD, TOOK ME TO BUY A NEW ONE

I stapled all my early minicomics with that stapler. *Sigh* But this new one is fine enough.

MARCH 12, 2007

SECRET POLICE

A basement!

Basements are ILLEGAL!

We didn't KNOW!

We're SORRY

We'll fill it IN!

PART OF AN EPIC NIGHTMARE↑   MARCH 13, 2007

BASEMENT

Snif, Snif

Hey, the skunk smell is gone.

Snif Snif

Still a slight odor coming up from the furnace vent

MARCH 13, 2007

FOUND IT!

AT THE POST OFFICE:

Have you guys seen my long neck stapler by any chance?

As a matter of fact... YES!

Now I have two!

Ha HA!

MARCH 14, 2007

HER CHARACTER

"I need a vacation from being so cute"

MARCH 15, 2007

STINKY BONES

ermf

The poo-poo lives in my bottom

It makes my bones so stinky!

MARCH 16, 2007

SNOW GHOSTS

Look, they're little GHOSTS!

No they're NOT! They're SNOWflakes.

ELI & MARIPOSA   MARCH 17, 2007

PRETTY AMY

When I grow up I'm going to marry a pretty girl and name her Amy.

You don't get to name her, she'll have her own name already.

Well, I'll just have to look until I find one named Amy.

I'll look up and down the WHOLE BLOCK!

MARCH 18, 2007

SPLASH

FOR THE LAST COUPLE OF YEARS I'VE BEEN STARING AT THE CEILING

TRYING TO DETERMINE IF THE WATER STAINS ARE STILL GETTING BIGGER OR NOT.

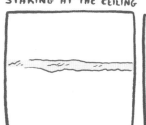

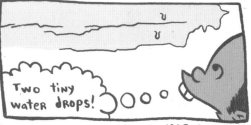
Two tiny water drops!

MARCH 19, 2007

NUMBER 5 IN BROWN

MARCH 20, 2007

BOOKSTORE COWBOY

Come on, Eli, we got to go home now

But

YOW!

What the FUCK Colin?!?

WUMP

You scared me!

I thought you were a crazy fan.

Ow

MARCH 21, 2007

ONE-BEER DIARY

Should I wait until after I draw my strip or should I drink this beer now?

Sweet sweet beer on the cob.

MARCH 22, 2007

UNTITLED

But Amy, it's very important for pregnant women to have sex as often as possible.

No it isn't, James.

Yes Amy, it IS!

MARCH 23, 2007

BEAVER POND

SPUT

Is it Rude to spit in Nature?

MARCH 24, 2007

ON THE COOKBOOK

YOGURT

PLOP

HOT GARLICKY OIL

FSSS

FRESH MINT, SALT & PEPPER, CAYENNE AND GRATED BOILED BEETS

BEET JUICE

OIL DROPLETS

YOGURT

MADHUR JAFFREY'S WORLD VEGETARIAN

MARCH 25, 2007

MONSTERFACE

ME AND ELI FOUND THIS NEAR THE SIDEWALK LAST FRIDAY NIGHT. I BROUGHT IT HOME TO DRAW...

SOME KIND OF PLUG.   MARCH 26, 2007

JASON'S CRUSH

How did the podcast go?

Pretty good.

But me & Jason got in a big FIGHT because he said he's NEVER had a CRUSH ON YOU.

I asked him if he had a CRUSH ON KERRIE, Creston's wife, and he said yeah.

That's bullshit. You're NOT good enough for him?

MARCH 27, 2007

UNDEAD

I'm so thirsty but I can't bear the thought of drinking water

I think I must have rabies.

You're probably just pregnant with a werewolf baby.

I've also been foaming at the mouth.

MARCH 28, 2007

JOKE WRITER

Listen. I wrote a new joke.

"How much is 2 plus 2?"

"FOUR"!

Ha Ha Ha ha!

That's math. Is math funny?

No. Yes!

DECLAN & ELI

MARCH 29, 2007

CRUMPLED ULTRASOUND

Amy, do you have the photo of our werewolf peanut?

I'll get it in a minute.

I need it NOW!

Here it is.

Hey it's all crumpled up!

Amy, it's all crumpled up!

That's just what happens.

MARCH 30, 2007

WEREWOLF PEANUT

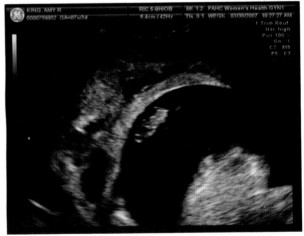

MARCH 30, 2007

DRAMATIC RE-ENACTMENT

Remember the other night, I was reading this book to you?

And I read "Stomp stomp stomp Sniff sniff sniff"

Achoo!

And then I said "That wasn't part of the story. I was Really Sneezing."

Ha ha ha

MARCH 31, 2007

NUGGING

You should give Amy a hug goodbye.

Guh

Jason said to hug you

Well, I hugged her. She cried a little and almost threw up.

Oh.

APRIL 1, 2007

MOTHER & WIFE

Eli

Please don't pile toys on top of me.

Eli! Don't pile toys on Momma!

She doesn't feel good!

APRIL 2, 2007

SOFT & SOUR

Well, goodnight sweetie.

KISS

I hate myself.

What?!

Why?

I'm just so sick

APRIL 3, 2007

MONSTER Mii

WITH THE NINTENDO Wii YOU CAN CREATE THESE LITTLE AVATARS CALLED Mii. I LIKE TO PUSH THE FACIAL FEATURES OUT OF THEIR REGULAR POSITIONS & MAKE STRANGE CREATURES

GLORVIX

ZANTHAR

SPEE ZAM

DORGIE

APRIL 4, 2007

FUCK EVERYTHING

THIS IS A COMIC ABOUT HOW ANGRY I AM.

Fucking Mario

HALF-WAY THROUGH COOKING DINNER THE OTHER NIGHT I GOT MAD, DECIDED IT WAS A STUPID DINNER, AND DUMPED IT IN THE TRASH, AND THEN STARTED OVER.

I don't want to eat this SHIT.

RANDOM HOUSE REJECTED MY AWESOME DRAGON PUNCHER BOOK AND THEY MIGHT BE GIANTS DOESN'T WANT MY BAND TO OPEN UP FOR THEM UP HERE AND ALL AMY DOES IS LIE ON THE COUCH AND MOAN.

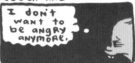

I don't want to be angry anymore.

I ERASE THIS COMIC SEVERAL TIMES AND START OVER FROM SCRATCH.

The trees are budding...

APRIL 5, 2007

LO MEIN

The baby worm is on his way to school when the daddy bird swoops down and catches him.

He flies back to the nest and feeds it to the baby bird.

ANGRY JASON

Cool, this shirt fits my new personality

I punch people in the FACE NOW!

APRIL 6, 2007

BUNNY TIME

Eli says the Easter Bunny is just a guy in a costume.

How do you know?

His eyes don't move and his mouth doesn't move.

LATER:

Hey, I think I might be the Easter Bunny!

I pooped and little rabbit-droppings came out.

APRIL 7, 2007

EASTER MORNING

I did it! I did it! I caught the EASTER BUNNY!

That's not the Easter Bunny.

What are you talking about? She's fluffy & brown isn't she?

The Easter Bunny is fluffy & WHITE.

What the HECK?

APRIL 8, 2007

BABY POISON

I need my Jamesy

Uhg. But not on my tummy.

That better?

Uh huh. Can you suck the poison from my neck?

SLURP

APRIL 9, 2007

Where are my gloves?

I just had them. What did I do with them?

Where did I put them?

Oh. They're in the bathroom sink!

APRIL 10, 2007

HIS MAJESTY'S REQUEST

Listen... Jason emailed music for a new song we're working on together.*

SOON
Do you want to hear it again?

Yeh!

And I want you to draw a comic about it too.

Draw a comic about listening to this music? I can do that.

* FOR PUNKY BREWSKIES   APRIL 11, 2007

OLIVES

Want to try one?

Yes

GAH!

POKE

ELI!

It was an accident!

GOD DAMN

Now there's dirt and hair all over them.

And olive oil on my pants.

APRIL 12, 2007

FRIDAY NIGHT COOKIES & BEER

Here comes Declan

POOF

Declan! Why did you blow out our candle?

I always do.

APRIL 13, 2007

AFTERNOON
QUICK STOP

Mommy!

mo mmeeee

I don't think I can cum while he's yelling "mommy"

APRIL 14, 2007

BLACK MAGIC

THE WAITRESSES WERE WITCHES!

EVERY BITE OF THE MAGIC FOOD THEY BROUGHT US PUT US TO SLEEP FOR A HUNDRED YEARS.

Z Zz

THE COOKS WERE WHITE WIZARDS. THEY WERE TRYING TO TURN THE WITCHES INTO FROGS AND THE WITCHES WERE TRYING TO TURN THEM INTO FROGS.

APRIL 15, 2007

KZORX

DOONGUS

DETHLIN

JAMES

APRIL 16, 2007

TAIL BONE

Did you know that people have tail bones?

My tail is in the front!

APRIL 16, 2007

BOSS BATTLE

I'm the boss of the whole level.

I think maybe you're just the mini-boss.

I'm NOT the MINI BOSS!

APRIL 17, 2007

TUBATOOB

What should we name the baby in Mama's tummy?

Tubatoob

Tubatoob? I don't think the baby would like that.

Oh, he'd get used to it.

It's a CUTE name.

APRIL 18, 2007

I STAYED UP LATE MAKING MORE Mii MONSTERS ON THE NINTENDO Wii AT THE REQUEST OF SWEDISH VIDEOGAME MAGAZINE +N

KLOOPIE

BLOOG

GLOG

ZEX

APRIL 19, 2007

MR. +N

AAAAAH!

WE TRIED TO TAKE OUT ELI'S SPLINTER BUT HE JUST WOULDN'T HOLD STILL.

AAAAAAH! AAH!

AFTER AN EXHAUSTING TWO HOUR BATTLE WE GAVE UP.

I just want to go to sleep.

Let's go to a Rock show

SO WE WENT TO SEE MY BAND, NOSE BLEED

NEW FAVORITE LOCAL ISLAND:

AAAAH!

APRIL 20, 2007

SUPERSPIN

Super Spin!

LATER Let me look at your thumb.

Hey! Part of your splinter fell out in the pool!

APRIL 21, 2007

MEMORIES OF THE DAY

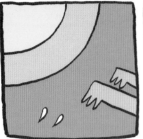 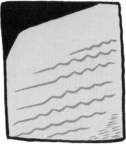

 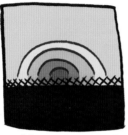

APRIL 22, 2007

LIFE OR DEATH

Unh... he got me, father

I will AVENGE you, SON!

CLANG!

Oh.

A dead animal.

You're RIGHT. I think it's a POSSUM.

APRIL 23, 2007

EXCEPT FOR THE DEMENTIA

How was the hospital?

I was IN the hospital?

Yeah, all week-end.

Hmm... the hospital?

Was I?

Oh yes! I was VERY well fed!

They also did a bunch of tests

They say you're incredibly healthy

That bodes well for you, when you get to be my age

SPRINGFIELD, VT

APRIL 24, 2007

ONE MORE STORY

That's NOT ENOUGH!

I will be CRANKY TOMORROW.

Don't be cranky, honey. If you're cranky, DADDY will be cranky.

And if daddy is cranky, SPANDY will be cranky.

APRIL 25, 2006

NICE THINGS

Do you say nice things to Amy?

You mean while we're having sex??

No. I say terrible, *terrible* things.

!!

APRIL 26, 2007

LIFE IS FULL OF SURPRISES

I PICKED UP MY PENCIL IN THE DARK

AND WHEN I TURNED ON THE LIGHT...

IT WAS THE WRONG PENCIL.

!!

APRIL 27, 2006

THE SWEET LIFE

Whenever I make lemon chicken, I like to make lemonade too.

When life gives you lemons, you make lemonade?

No... life never gives me "lemons"

I mean, nothing SOUR ever happens to me.

Yeah...

Life gives you peaches

And you make Rotten peaches

1 lb of chicken, cut in chunks
The juice of 2 or 3 lemons
Fresh garlic & ginger
Soy sauce & brown sugar

APRIL 28, 2007

DISCOMBOBULATE

Let me turn off the discombobulater.

CLICK

Say "discombobulater".

discombobulater

You can say it!

How did you used to say it?

discombobu-banana!

APRIL 29, 2007

MAPLE PEOPLE

YESTERDAY AT THE MAPLE FESTIVAL, GOING AROUND AND AROUND...

THERE'S So many people at the maple festival!

And everyone is happy

OR ANGRY

...OR BORED, OR SAD, OR...

KATE'S SWE

APRIL 30, 2007

FLASH

WHILE HOLDING MY SKETCHBOOK, WATCHING TV, GETTING READY TO DRAW TODAY'S STRIP

!!!

Amy, I suddenly can Remember all sorts of things about when I was in PRE-School

I can remember walking down the stairs to the potty all by myself.

Great! You can tell me all about it tomorrow

MAY 1, 2007

INTERVIEW
WITH CHANNEL 3 NEWS

Why is the microphone so little

Eli, don't pick your nose on T.V.
whoops

When you wiggle my brush goes in the WRONG direction!
I just got surprised

MAY 2, 2007

MY NEIGHBOR PROVIDES
EXTRA INFORMATION

Oh, I have to tell you something
Oh, yes?

I Read your strip in the paper about the possum...

It died under my porch and I carried it down there with a snow shovel!
Oh, that's GREAT!

MAY 3, 2007

LIVING THE GAME

Don't forget to drink some water...
You have to control me

I'll press the drink button.
"PRESS"

Now press the drink button for me.

Drink faster!
"PRESS" "PRESS" "PRESS"

AT STONE SOUP

MAY 4, 2007

SEXY TUMMY

I think I pulled my tummy muscles last night

why am I so weak?

Amy, I'm going to start doing sit-ups so I can make love to you better.
Uh...
alright

MAY 5, 2007

TINY MOON

THE FIRST OBJECT TO APPEAR IN THE TWILIGHT SKY...

"THAT'S THE TINIEST MOON I EVER SAW" I SAID, AND WE ALL LAUGHED. MAY 5, 2007

HEART OF BASS

THE MUFFLED BASS FROM THE SOUND SYSTEM OF A PASSING CAR AS HE FALLS ASLEEP

boompf boompf boompf

Boompf Boompf boompf

MAKING PLANS WITH PISTOL

when I come visit you in San Francisco, I'll draw you in my strip...

maaaaybe.

MAY 6, 2007

HOT NAP

Oh, sweetie

There's a little puddle of sweat inside your ear.

MAY 11, 2007

CROSSING THE STREET

I WAS CROSSING THE STREET...

THIS WHITE VAN WAS NOT SLOWING DOWN OR STOPPING FOR ME...

SO I HIT IT WITH MY UMBRELLA AS IT PASSED

WUNK

MAY 12, 2007

MOTHER'S DAY

ELI TOOK A QUARTER OUT OF HIS MOMMA'S POCKET.
Hey!

LATER WE FOUND A GLASS FOR 25¢ AT A YARD SALE.
Do you still have that quarter you found?
You could use it to buy Momma this glass.

TODAY WE WOKE UP AND MADE SOME ORANGE LEMONADE

WHICH ELI CARRIED VERY CAREFULLY.
Look, Momma!

MAY 13, 2007

COMIC STREP

I'M HAVING AN IMPOSSIBLE TIME REMEMBERING MY ANTIBIOTICS.
Did I take my pill yet?
Amy?!

I HAD BEEN REDUCED TO CONSTANTLY RE-COUNTING THE PILLS TO SEE IF I'D TAKEN THEM.
There's 24 pills left. Does that mean I took one this morning or not?

SO AMY CAME UP WITH THIS IDEA TO PUT THE THREE PILLS FOR THE DAY IN A CUP EACH MORNING.

BUT... NOW I FORGET TO LOOK IN THE CUP.

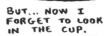

MAY 14, 2007

LIFE AND DEATH

Are you alive or dead?

Alive. ♪Ding ding ding♪ Right answer.

Are you living or dying?

I'm living

♪dUN-duhn♪ WRONG answer.

MAY 15, 2007

COLD SORES

"Hello!"

"I'm my sore!"

MAY 16, 2007

TOY FALL

Well Mom... you and Dad could always move in with us.

CRUNCH

OW!

MAY 17, 2007

ANY OTHER COMICS

MAKING PLANS:

When the baby comes I'll take eight weeks off from work.

Then you could take a few months off from drawing until my summer vacation

Sure... well, I'd still have to draw my diary strip...

You can draw the diary strip and take care of the baby. But take a sabbatical from working on any other comics, right?

MAY 18, 2007

HUGS

AT THE FIRST COMMENCEMENT CEREMONY FOR THE CENTER FOR CARTOON STUDIES.

Congratulations

LATER You hugged Josie but NOT Elizabeth!

Oh shit. That was mean.

MAY 19, 2007

VENON

Eli invented this supervillian named VENON who pees blood... and whose body is covered with penises and vulvas!

Eli did!?

And tell her about your movie idea... "Big in the Tummy"

Alex is a big boy an' he's still in his momma's tummy

And when he comes out his momma says "Alex!"

MAY 20, 2007

THE SELF

THEY SAY THAT FOR EVERY ONE "HUMAN" CELL THE BODY IS HOST TO TEN BACTERIA.

AFTER A TEN DAY COURSE OF ANTI-BIOTICS, I FEEL HOLLOW AND EMPTY

LIKE A BALLOON

OR A ROTTEN LOG

MAY 21, 2007

TOO BLUE

The sky is too blue.

It's kind of oppressive.

MAY 22, 2007

SQUEEKY PEEPY

I just don't think we can take care of a baby bird.

You could put him back up in the tree... maybe he would fall asleep and have sweet dreams about his momma before he dies.

Squeek Squeek

MAY 23, 2007

JACKSON'S MAGAZINES

flip flip

?

Dave! Which issue of PEOPLE writes about Alec Baldwin's divorce?

(AMY'S BROTHER'S HOUSE)

MAY 24, 2007

CRAZY WOOD

So, we picked out crazy new hardwood floors today.

"Brazilian Hickory" *

DUNBAR

Oh yeah, rainforest wood? It was probably harvested by slaves

What!?

* GUAJAVIRA

MAY 25, 2007

FORTY!

AT MY 40TH BIRTHDAY BAGLE BRUNCH

Jason has never come to one of my birthday parties ever.

why do you think that is?

Well...

He says he hates bagels because they're "pretentious" and he thinks such early parties are "stupid."

But it's really because he hates me!

MAY 26, 2007

TOM & PEGGY & THEIR LI'L KIDS MISSED MY
BIRTHDAY YESTERDAY SO THEY'RE COMING TODAY

LUNG WHISTLE

I'M SORRY YOU'RE
SICK, ELI

It's okay.
I like it.

I like it when
my lungs whistle.

♪

That was Peggy
on the phone...
they're just leaving
Montreal NOW

Did you warn
her that Eli's
sick?

No... Do you
think she'll
be mad?

when
Peggy gets
here, pretend
you're
not sick!

MAY 27, 2007

LIVES OF THE LIVING

WALKING PAST THE GRAVEYARD, THEY
CHOOSE BABY NAMES FROM THE TOMBSTONES

I'M THE
BOSS!!

AAARGH.

HANNAH'S
NICE.

ELIZA.

HENRIETTA
ELIZA
KOCHALKA.

Magic
Wands!

ARG

Boom!

*GUEST DRAWING
BY TOM DEVLIN

MAY 28, 2007

LITTLE BOX WITH STARS

GETTING EVERYTHING OUT OF THE BEDROOM
SO WE CAN PUT IN THE NEW FLOORS.

James, what's
this?

Oh... that's the box
from a little
chocolate I gave
Momma back near
when I first
met her.

There's NO
chocolate in
it NOW, though.

MAY 29, 2007

WORKERS

PUTTING IN OUR NEW FLOORS

BAM

VVVVV

I KNOW...
what's his
Name? That
guy?

Patrick?

He's
YOUR
COUSIN

I KNOW Patrick
but I don't
KNOW that
other one.

That's Uncle
Kevin.

Oh.

MAY 30, 2007

AUTOMATIC DADDY

Pick me up

Wait. How did you get in my arms?

You picked me up.

I did?

MAY 31, 2007

CALL OF THE WILD

NOW I'M HAPPY WHEN THE PHONE RINGS

BECAUSE I HAVE A NEW PHONECORD!

RING

Oh Boy!

RING

THE OLD CORD USED TO DISCONNECT CALLS IF YOU WIGGLED IT. I NEVER GOT AROUND TO REPLACING IT, SO A LOT OF CALLS GOT DISCONNECTED. I FINALLY JUST GOT LUCKY AND FOUND A REPLACEMENT LYING OUTSIDE ON THE GROUND SOMEWHERE.

Oh! We need one of those!

JUNE 1, 2007

STUPID PUNISHMENT

Eli! Close your eyes and TRY to go to sleep!

No.

If you won't take a nap then you can sit in TIME OUT instead.

Wait a minute... That's a stupid PUNISHMENT.

JUNE 2, 2007

THE UNDRAWABLE FLOOR

EVERY BOARD IS COMPLETELY DIFFERENT

Patrick and Kevin will come back this week to do your floor too.

And then I will love you, and we will live happily ever after ♪♪

JUNE 3, 2007

NOT JUST THE TOES

 SORRY I NEVER REALLY TALK TO YOU ANYMORE.

Eh. It's okay.

But could you rub the _whole_ foot?

RUB

JUNE 4, 2007

LETTERS OF LOVE

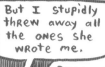 Amy still has all the old love letters I sent her.

 But I stupidly threw away all the ones she wrote me.

Once we moved in together I figured I didn't need them.

 Amy, this old dress of yours is stained. Can I throw it away?

 James, that's my WEDDING DRESS!

JUNE 5, 2007

PODCAST!

IT TOOK LIKE A MONTH BUT IT'S FINALLY READY

 Here's the podcast

wrapped in newspaper

 I'm fuckin' tired. I'm going home.

JUNE 6, 2007

HOT SUSHI

 That's my friend Atsushi

Hot Sushi!?

That can't possibly be your real name? Can it?

???

Yeah

JUNE 7, 2007

COLD SHIT

 Is he going to be the first "person of color" in your strip"?

Well...there was this African guy who spoke French that I played Boggle with

But he lost 'cause he didn't know English

DRUNK IN SAN FRAN   JUNE 7, 2007

LONG DISTANCE BEDTIME STORIES

The Joker stole Batman's boot and hid it in a tree

So Batman hopped through the forest on one foot chopping down all the trees with his axe.

JUNE 8, 2007

OPENING

... the paintings are peeling up.

Oh... huh. It's the humidity

what's that?

wet air.

Awake to Stellina uprit
& WHAT DID I JUST WRITE DRUNK?

JUNE 9, 2007

SOJU MORNING

I think I feel it this time

Oh yeah? That last soju was GIANT!

Your hair looks cool in the morning.

PISTOL'S APARTMENT IN SAN FRANCISCO

JUNE 10, 2007

MARSHMALLOW CLOUDS

Attack the MARSHMALLOW!

JUNE 10, 2007

SNUGGER

Eli said you were gonna "snuggle our socks off" when you got home

JUNE 11, 2007

TIME ZONE

ARRANGING MY PAINTINGS FOR A BOOK COLLECTION.

Geez! It's one a.m.

I've been working pratically NON-STOP since 7:30 this morning.

I was having so much FUN.

JUNE 12, 2007

FREE GUNK

I scraped some gunk off my tongue and fed it to these ants.

They like gunk?

JUNE 13, 2007

DRAWING THE FIRST PANEL OF TODAY'S STRIP I SUDDENLY BECAME HYPER-AWARE OF THE ACT OF DRAWING.

JUNE 14, 2007

WIDE ASLEEP

Look, Amy. He's sleeping with his eyes wide open.

I guess he's too tired to shut them

Z

LATER

Eli, don't you want to wake up from your nap?

It's almost time for BED!

Z

JUNE 15, 2007

BROWN EYES

I grabbed some free samples at the farmers market to feed the duck.

Look, she's got brown eyes, just like you and mommy!

JUNE 16, 2007

STRAWBERRY LIGHTNING

We might not want to pick strawberries tomorrow, if it rains.

Yeah, you might get electrocuted!

You'd hold up the strawberry and say "look what I found"

Then lightning strikes and ZZZT!

Straw- berry Jam!

JUNE 17, 2007

PENIS

Did you see that, Eli?!

The baby waved at you.

Oops! It sure looks like a boy!

There's no hiding that

JUNE 18, 2007

LEARNING A NEW SONG AT

BAND PRACTICE

WAIT, WAIT. That's not right.

That's how you just sang it to us

Well, I sing it a little different every time.

I know!

JUNE 19, 2007

HAT LOSER

MY BEST HAT WAS RED & WHITE

AND IT ALSO LIKED TO FIGHT

RAR!

I LOST MY BEST HAT, LATE ONE NIGHT*

* ACTUALLY, IT WAS IN THE AFTERNOON

WHEN I LEFT IT AT THE BEACH.*

* I THINK

JUNE 20, 2007

BOOMERANG

JUST MINUTES AFTER I POSTED YESTERDAY'S STRIP

Guess what I found while riding my bicycle to work?

I wasn't sure it was yours but I figured it had to be...

Oh, that's so great!

You might want to wash it before you wear it. It's filthy.

JUNE 21, 2007

BLOODY GUITAR

look at this

You gotta draw about this

Dude, I saw on "Dateline" that that kind of blood-splatter can only be caused by a GUNSHOT WOUND!

AFTER THE ROCK SHOW

JUNE 22, 2007

IN A YELLOW POTTY

SURROUNDED BY THE VIBRANT GREEN OF THE NORTHEAST KINGDOM, THE BRIGHT BLUE CHEMICAL FLUID MIXES WITH SHIT AND PISS.

ew

Do you want to stand up or sit down?

sit down

I hope he doesn't fall in.

WEST BURKE, VT

JUNE 23, 2007

GOODNIGHT SANDWICH

AFTER THE EVENS CONCERT, ELI WAS HUNGRY SO AMY MADE HIM A SANDWICH

Eli! You're eating your sandwich too slow

I need to go to bed

It's 11:15! He's been eating that sandwich for an hour.

Eli! Finish your sandwich!

JUNE 24, 2007

SUMMER RAIN

I'm making it RAIN!

Not Right at me! Up in the air!

ELI TOOK OFF HIS WET CLOTHES BEFORE HIS NAP BUT THEN I COULDN'T RESIST TRYING TO PICK AT THE WEIRD BUMPS ON HIS BACK WHILE HE SLEPT.

Hmm... they're not pimples

JUNE 25, 2007

HOT FREAKS

Mud

Do you like my nipples?

NORTH BEACH

JUNE 26, 2007

PERVERT

WHILE AMY READ A STORY TO ELI, I LOOKED AT HER CROTCH

I SEE A MOSQUITTO ABOUT TO BITE

SLAP

Ow!

JUNE 27, 2007

FIRE FLY

WE STAYED UP LATE TO SEE FIREFLIES

There's one on your head

Ha ha! Eek!

Now it's on your EYE!

Oh!

AND FLYING IN THE NIGHT WIND

Aah!

JUNE 28, 2007

LIFE VS. DEATH

Daddy! I can't see you!

CAN YOU SEE MY HAT?!

Look Eli, I found it!

That old dead POSSUM

There's a piece of grass growing from its eye socket

why?

JUNE 29, 2007

NATIONAL ANTHEM

WHEN THE NATIONAL ANTHEM PLAYS, MY HEART SWELLS WITH EMOTION.

THEN I IMAGINE THE BASEBALL PLAYERS GETTING THEIR LEGS BLOWN OFF IN IRAQ

EARLIER:

I think my bottom's broken

It's got a CRACK in it.

JUNE 30, 2007

ORANGE JUICE

Stop being mean to me or I'll SMASH this box of orange juice.

Eli, if Mamma is mean to me I want you to throw the orange juice down and smash it

Don't smash the orange juice!

I won't really

12TH ANNIVERSARY

JULY 1, 2007

SMUGGLE TUMMY

Do you think they'll accuse me of trying to steal a bowling ball when we leave?

ELI: 55 AMY: 57 JAMES: 83   JULY 1, 2007

SALT WINE

I wonder if it's possible to make salty wine? SALT WINE could be my GREATEST INVENTION!

JULY 2, 2007

BUBBLE WATER

Mama!

Eli! Be careful!

SSSS SELTZER

Do you like bubble tables?

JULY 3, 2007

AMERICA'S ELF

LEAVING THE FIREWORKS EARLY

BOOM KAPOW

The fireworks are fine and all... I like 'em

but IRAQ kinda takes all the fun out of the fourth of July.

(LAST NIGHT)   JULY 4, 2007

FLAUNT IT

Let me see your breasts

Stop it!

They're mine and they're not for showing everyone.

But Mama, they're beautiful!

JULY 5, 2007

BEE STORY

Did you ever hear of bees that fly in your ear and make honey from your ear wax?

But the honey is yucky so they throw it on the floor

KOCHALKA POWER

WE WERE ALL STICKING UTENSILS TO OUR FACES

I bet we could do these glasses if we made the right suction with our cheeks.

Yeah!

I've got to show the waitress

Mmm! Mmm!

MONHEGAN ISLAND   JULY 9, 2007

SHELL CRUSHER JOB

CRUNCH

Want to come in my office, Mama?

MONHEGAN ISLAND   JULY 10, 2007

SCREAMING INTO THE FOG, UP BY THE LIGHTHOUSE

DAY-O

DAY-AY-AY AY-AY-AY -AY-AY-AY Oh

We shook the mountain!

We shook the MOUNTAIN WITH SONG! *

MONHEGAN ISLAND   JULY 11, 2007
* NOT REALLY A MOUNTAIN

SEXY GIRL

Amy, you've got three nipples!

haRumph

KISS

Your face smells like LOBSTER!

Sorry

MONHEGAN ISLAND   JULY 11, 2007

FISH KISSER

Look, Eli.

It's a Pollack, Eli. Want to touch it?

Can I kiss it?

KISS

Amy! I licked a Piccasso* and now I've kissed a Pollock!

MONHEGAN ISLAND
*(DESMOISELLES D'AVIGNON)

JULY 12, 2007

FIRST KISS

ELI GAVE HIS LITTLE COUSIN JORDAN A VERY ROMANTIC KISS.

!!!

MONHEGAN

JULY 13, 2007

LANDSCAPES

EVERYWHERE YOU GO ON MONHEGAN ISLAND, SOMEONE IS PAINTING PICTURES

This is my painting of Whitehead and this is Gull Rock and..

Ooh, very good. But the waves are quite "cartoony". Maybe you could fix it....

You're so competitive. Why do you care if you're a better landscape painter than some old ladies?

You should've said "I'm only painting landscapes to MAKE FUN OF YOU"

MONHEGAN ISLAND

JULY 13, 2007

MR. WATERY

TURNING SAD INTO HAPPY

The "Kid's fit meal" comes with a "kid's fit toy" but it doesn't say what the toy is.

That's okay, James. I will be happy with whatever they give to me.

FIT MEAL

Now let's see what the toy—

—a water bottle!?

Oh! Honey, I see the tears welling up in your eyes.

BUT, SOON:

"Hi, I'm Watery. Look what I can do!" ♪♪

"I'm Appley"

WEST LEBANON, NH

JULY 14, 2007

HYPER STRIPES

This guy is too powerful!

Hyper Stripes! We need your help!

Aah!

NOODLE ARMS

STRONG FIST

Get him, HYPER STRIPES! BLAM!

JULY 15, 2007

BLACK RASPBERRY

Blackberries

Let's pretend we live in the woods and this is the only food we have to eat.

THEN WE SEE A HOMELESS GUY HUNCHED OVER, SHAKING FROM THE D.T.'S, EATING BERRIES TOO...

JULY 16, 2007

ARROW BOY

I CUT A COUPLE BRANCHES OFF THE TREE TO MAKE ELI A BOW AND ARROW

FWIP

FWUP

TUNK

JULY 17, 2007

BLUEBERRY LASER

Will you help me draw my comic strip? You could draw yourself picking blueberries

No.

I want to draw a HERO shooting the blueberry bush with his LASERS!

JULY 18, 2007

ON TURNING FOUR

I don't know what it looks like to be four.

I think maybe my face will be different.

JULY 19, 2007

LITTLE BLACK MIC

JASON CAME OVER TO HELP RECORD A ROUGH DEMO WITH ME FOR THAT DISNEY SHOW

Hey! Is this my microphone?

Yeah... I think you GAVE it to me.

oh

Well... you can have it back.

It might be broken

BUT HE FORGOT THE MICROPHONE WHEN HE LEFT.

JULY 20, 2007

OVER SHADOWED

MY HOME TOWN OF SPRINGFIELD VT WAS NAMED THE OFFICIAL HOME OF THE SIMPSONS AND HOSTED THE MOVIE'S WORLD PREMIERE THERE TODAY.

D'oh

Now Springfield will NEVER be known as the birthplace of James Kochalka.

LATER

Wait... I wasn't born there.

JULY 21, 2007

EN FRANÇAIS

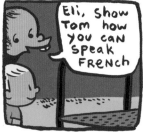

Eli, show Tom how you can speak FRENCH

blaplabfbleblah

MONTREAL

That's rather disrespectful of FRENCH culture

Tom! You're hurting his feelings!

JULY 22, 2007

★ JUST FOR KICKS ★

WAKE UP, BABY BROTHER!

MONTREAL

He kicked again! Did you see it?

Yay!

JULY 23, 2007

STRESS

The stove thing is falling off.

It's not being held on by anything!

Get something to PROP this up! I've got a conference call with DISNEY RIGHT NOW!

(THANKS ALAN, FOR COMING OVER TO FIX IT.)

JULY 24, 2007

MONHEGAN SPLINTER

No No No!

There. It's out! It's a tiny peice of Monhegan Island.

Oh!

Shall I tape it into my sketchbook?

The sketchbook will scream "Ouch! I've got a splinter!"

Ha ha

JULY 25, 2007

SPECTACULAR

AMY'S GOT THE MOST SPECTACULAR BODY ON THE WHOLE BEACH

JULY 26, 2007

SIMPSONS

WE WENT TO SPRINGFIELD, VT TO WATCH THE SIMPSONS MOVIE WITH MY PARENTS, BUT WHEN IT WAS OVER:

That's it?? Just a cartoon?

When does the Real movie start?

That was the movie.

We paid FIVE DOLLARS for that?!

JULY 27, 2007

DRIED OUT

Geez, I hardly drink any alcohol anymore.

My brother's got high cholesterol. I should drink alcohol to keep my veins clean of cholesterol.

But... alcohol supposedly also encourages the growth of new blood vessels... which can help cancers grow faster.

My throat feels dry

JULY 28, 2007

GETTING SEXIER

Have you Noticed I'm SEXIER than I've EVER BEEN?

TUG

Yeah

Well..? Don't you just want to Lick me FROM HEAD to TOE?

It sounds like a lot of work.

JULY 29, 2007

STINKY PILE

Amy... this pile of clothes stinks

I'll take care of it later

I don't believe you.

LATER Don't take it NOW! I'm DRAWING it!

JULY 30, 2007

WILD CAT

HISS

Oh, shush.

Just because you got outside for five minutes doesn't mean you're a WILD animal now.

Just because you chased those kitties away and puffed up like a puffer fish doesn't mean you can hiss at everyone in your family...

LATER

I think Spandy WON that battle!

JULY 31, 2007

HOT NIGHT

8, 8, 9, 8

9, 8, 8, 9

9, 9, 8, 8, 9

8, 8, 9, 8, 9

WHAT IS HE DOING? I'M NOT SURE.

AUGUST 1, 2007

KNOWLEDGE

"Poo" is P-O-O. "PEE" is spelled P-E-E.

Now you try.

That sorta looks like a "P." Good job. Now go show Momma.

Momma!

Poo PEE

IS POWER

ALL YEAR I'VE BEEN TELLING ELI HE'D LEARN TO SWIM WHEN HE TURNED FOUR. NOW, A FEW WEEKS BEFORE HIS BIRTHDAY, HE WAS READY TO TRY.

I can swim without a floaty thing now!

AUGUST 2, 2007

RYKO-WOOOOOSH

CLICK

Well, Ryko just dropped me.

Are you upset?

Actually, I feel HAPPY!

Giddy, even!

AUGUST 3, 2007

HUMAN WEALTH

YESTERDAY BILLY FROM RYKODISC ASKED ME HOW MY COMICS CAREER WAS GOING

Pretty good. I'm making a living but I'm not getting rich.
I go to the beach every day

You go to the BEACH every day? Dude, you ARE rich.

TODAY STU TOOK US OUT TUBING

WAAA

AUGUST 4, 2007

PERPENDICULAR

ON A FOLD-OUT COUCH AT MY SISTER'S HOUSE

If I sleep this way and you sleep that way, where will Daddy sleep?

On the ceiling.
Hee hee

ANTRIM, NH

AUGUST 5, 2007

SHY, SHY, SUPERSTAR

LAST NIGHT AT MY NEPHEW PATRICK'S 21st BIRTHDAY PARTY, SOME OF THE GIRLS WANTED TO HEAR ME SING A SONG.

This is a new song that I haven't recorded yet.
um...

Beyoncé you can't handle me, you can't hold a candle to a man like me, you can't even jiggle my handle, see? 'cause I more than a handful be. ♫

ANTRIM, NH   AUGUST 6, 2007

FLIRT

I'm wearing your favorite shorts*

Oh, good. I'll make love to you tonight.
Well...

Do you think you could give me a nice long back-rub first?
Sure!

—with my DICK!
♫ Oh, Dickie.

* ACTUALLY PANTIES   AUGUST 7, 2007

UPSIDE DOWN ANIMALS

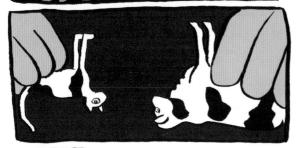

"mee-ooo"

And what does upside-down cow say?

Moo-ow

AUGUST 8, 2007

JOHN CARTER OF MARS
...LIES BLEEDING TO DEATH, BOTH LEGS CUT OFF...

We have come to take over MARS!

No! I live here

hee hee hee

Why are you laughing?

Because you boys are SO FUNNY

AUGUST 9, 2007

CALLING KITTIES IN THE DARK

Spandy ♫

Here kitty kitty kitty

♫ kiss kiss kiss kiss ♫

RUSTLE

hello cutie

Oh!

AUGUST 10, 2007

SECRET RECEIPT

James! James! I found a Receipt in my Room.

And look what it has on it: ULTRAMANS!

It must be a CLUE!

!?

HIS BIRTHDAY'S COMING SOON

AUGUST 11, 2007

CRUSTWICH

Do you want a crustwich

What's a crustwich?

It's a sandwich made using just the crust. You'll love it.

AUGUST 12, 2007

S G F R T

..certified letter for James—

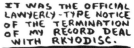

IT WAS THE OFFICIAL LAWYERLY-TYPE NOTICE OF THE TERMINATION OF MY RECORD DEAL WITH RKYODISC.

RYKO

AUGUST 13, 2007

WATCHING WATER

Look at the water

It's splashing me!

Cool

Let's pretend we're watching television.

Okay

RED ROCKS

AUGUST 14, 2007

FAMILY PROJECT

BUILDING MY DRESSER FROM IKEA

Here, you can finish the nail

TAP TAP TAP

There, it's done. Eli can sleep in the bottom drawer, Mommy can sleep in the middle drawer, and Daddy can sleep in the top drawer.

AUGUST 15, 2007

GET DRESSED

LAST NIGHT, WHEN WE WENT TO ANDREA'S FOR DINNER, ELI WANTED TO GO IN COSTUME

TONIGHT WE WORE OUR PAJAMAS TO THE LULLATONE CONCERT.

AUGUST 16, 2007

HEAD PUNCHER

PUNCH PUNCH PUNCH

Stop! If you hit yourself ONE more time, I'll hit DADDY.

KLONK

Hit HiM HARD!

hey

HIT

AUGUST 17, 2007

WILD PARTY

Alright kids, listen up.

No one break the T.V.

KLONK

Don't break the Wii either!

AUGUST 18, 2007

GRANDMA'S TEETH

Alright, I'll look for them.

Hi Mom

I found them in the garbage.

Well... they weren't too deep.

AUGUST 19, 2007

TODAY'S ADVENTURE

WE CROSSED THE BRIDGE OF DOOM

CREAK

PAST FIVE SERPENTS

Aah!

TO SEE THE GRAFFITI UNDER THE HIGHWAY

Momma, it was so cool.

I found a bullet

AUGUST 20, 2007

DANIEL FUNK

ALL SUMMER LONG I'VE BEEN WORKING ON THIS THEMESONG FOR A DISNEY CARTOON SHOW

who shrunk who shrunk Daniel FUNK

Is Daniel Funk real?

what do you mean?

TONIGHT WE FINALLY GOT DOWN TO RECORDING IN EARNEST. I LAUGHED MYSELF SILLY WHILE JASON MOCK-DRUMMED ALONG WITH JEREMY'S REAL DRUMS.

CRASH

BOOM

AUGUST 21, 2007

PURE POP

TALKING TO HERB AT THE RECORD STORE WHILE ELI LISTENS TO CDS AT THE LISTENING STATION

So, I sent Disney our first demo a few weeks ago...

but they accused me of trying to "sell out" to them

They asked if I could make it more "James Kochalka"

That's so funny!

So for the NEW versions, I made them on my GameBoy using a program called Nanoloop, and then we're adding rock instruments on top

AUGUST 22, 2007

4 IN A BED

You boys were kicking me all Night!

The baby was kicking, Eli was kicking, and Daddy was kicking too

Eli dreamt he stepped in cat puke.

He said "Momma wipe my foot off"!

I dreamt that Eli was Samus from Metroid and he took his robot suit off in the bed. I was mad that he was going to lose a screw.

You kept saying "push the button to fire the missiles"

AUGUST 23, 2007

THE SEA GARK

THE SEA GARK HAS A BODY LIKE A MAN AND A FACE LIKE A SEAL. SOMETIMES THEY HAVE A CLAW LIKE A LOBSTER. ONE LIVES IN LAKE CHAMPLAIN, AND SOMETIMES YOU CAN SEE A WHITE SPLASH OF WATER WHEN HE STICKS HIS NOSE OUT OF THE WATER TO CATCH A BREATH.

There, did you see it?!

In a hundred years all the kids will know the Sea Gark and they'll forget "Champ"*

You're gonna just keep trying until something sticks, aren't you

*THE OTHER LAKE MONSTER

AUGUST 24, 2007

AN INCONVENIENT TRUTH

I think I need another haircut already

Your hair looks good

No it doesn't, it's all bald.

That's just your ice-cap melting.

AUGUST 25, 2007

REFLECTION

How does it feel to be on vacation without momma?

AND WITH A GIGGLE HE SAID:

Pretty Strange

LAKE HEWITT

AUGUST 26, 2007

NAMING SOMETHING

I want to Name him Sucky

I want to Name him Bloody

Hey everbody! We caught a LEECH!

LAKE HEWITT

AUGUST 27, 2007

RELEASE

MY CHILDREN'S BOOK "SQUIRRELLY GRAY" COMES OUT TODAY, BUT THE LOCAL BOOKSTORES DON'T HAVE IT.

ALSO, METROID PRIME 3 CAME OUT TODAY FOR THE NINTENDO Wii

Momma might not like all the shooting...

Tell mamma it's not scary... it's exciting!

AUGUST 28, 2007

BUMPS

THE OTHER DAY I TAUGHT ELI ABOUT THE PIMPLY PINE TREES THAT GROW ON TOP OF THE MOUNTAIN THAT OVERLOOKS LAKE HEWITT.

Poke it with the Stick

SQUIRT

I think I got some in my mouth.

A FEW MINUTES LATER A WASP STUNG MY BALD SPOT. TODAY IT ITCHES.

AUGUST 29, 2007

FRIDGE BOX

I BOUGHT BEER FOR THE BAND TO DRINK WHILE WE RECORD:

Ow

MILLER Lite

The cardboard went up under my finger Nail!

Let me show you how a REAL man does it

ermf

MILLER Lite

Arg

MILLER Lite

AUGUST 30, 2007

BUMPIN'

I keep telling Amy that she's cute and sexy but she says she's not.

she is

Hey, you two should "bump tummies"!

heh heh

hurrr...

BUMP

AUGUST 31, 2007

ALL OUR FRIENDS GO TO THE SATURDAY FARMER'S MARKET

I've got some crazy news...

I was offered a kinda big part in a feature film. I go to Austin, Texas next weekend to shoot it.

I'm not even really an actor!

I wonder if there's any other friends around here to brag to...

I'm gonna do my scenes with PARIS from THE GILMORE GIRLS! I'm so freaked out!

What if she HATES me?

SEPTEMBER 1, 2007

METROID SURPRISE

Zzz

Will you wake up and play METROID?

Snort?

Will you wake up and play METROID PRIME? ♫

Well, my hand hurts from playing too much

but...

YES!

SEPTEMBER 2, 2007

PROTESTING EVERYTHING

Toot!

James!? Why are you in this protest?

It's the LABOR DAY parade!

SEPTEMBER 3, 2007

ALL AROUND THE WOOD PILE

Hey, there's wood on THIS side too!

SEPTEMBER 4, 2007

ON THE COB

AT DINNER LAST NIGHT

Did you ever eat potato on the cob?

No

Want to try it? Let's try it.

I'll put some potato on your CORN COB

Are we going to eat everything "ON the cob" NOW?

Will we drink water on the cob?

COB ON the COB!

SEPTEMBER 5, 2007

MOVIE MOVIE

I SHAVED THE BUSHY WHITE HAIRS THAT GROW IN MY EARS

Ow

READ THE MOVIE SCRIPT FOR "MARS"

STARTED LEARNING MY LINES...

Space travel sounds about as exciting as... solitary confinement in a motel room in Winnepeg

I wonder if I should order some toys online? Then even if I die in a plane crash, Eli would get one last present from me.

SEPTEMBER 6, 2007

ANTICRASH

The plane was broken so I couldn't fly away today.

I don't think you should fly away if the plane is broken

That's why I came back home.

SEPTEMBER 7, 2007

HER CLOSEUP

SHOOTING A MOVIE IN AN OLD AIRCRAFT-HANGER, IN FRONT OF A GIANT GREEN SCREEN

I'm aware of every little movement my face makes

AUSTIN, TEXAS Shooting "MARS"

SEPTEMBER 8, 2007

THE NIGHT WAS MINE

AT ALMOST FOUR IN THE MORNING WE FINISHED!
I HUGGED MY DIRECTOR — AND MY ACTRESS

Ha!

my actress

AS WE WALKED BACK TO OUR TRAILERS
WE LOOKED OUT OVER THE AUSTIN HORIZON

Look... a giant Christmas tree

*
.....

* LIZA SAYS SOMETHING
I DON'T HEAR. MY
ACTRESS!

SEPTEMBER 9, 2007

BACK FROM MARS

WHEN I CAME HOME FROM THE PLANE
LAST NIGHT, EVERYONE WAS ASLEEP

TODAY, AMY CALLED FROM WORK:

Mary wants to know if you had an affair with your "Gilmore Girl"

Ehn. It was hard to tell if she wanted to!

SEPTEMBER 10, 2007

WONDERFULL

WHEN THE RAIN COMES, ME AND ELI LIKE
TO LIE ON THE FLOOR OF HIS BEDROOM
AND LISTEN TO THE RAIN HIT HIS SKYLIGHT.

SEPTEMBER 11, 2007

EEEEEEEEEEEEEEELI

WAAAA

What's WRONG??

Eli wrote you an email of all E's. He didn't want to send it but I sent it to you anyway

WAAA

I didn't think he'd notice that I clicked "send"

I wan to read it... let me check my email

No! I won't let you have it!

Hey! You pressed DELETE!

SEPTEMBER 12, 2007

THE CLOSED MOUTH

Open your mouth.
NN

Open your mouth.

Alright, I'm taking your toys away.

Which toys should I take away?

SEPTEMBER 13, 2007

CALLING MY MOM

Wait. Listen to this

SSS

Did you hear that? It's Eli peeing.

SEPTEMBER 14, 2007

KOCHALKA ORIGINAL

Make me a kitty

There

Now you're one of my drawings

(YESTERDAY)

SEPTEMBER 15, 2007

LITTLE KID ROCK SHOW

DID A ROCK SHOW LAST NIGHT, ONE TODAY

READ MY BOOK CALLED SQUIRRELLY GRAY

ALL THE CHILDREN JUMPED & PLAYED

INSIDE, MY HEART IT THUMPS HOORAY

It's hard to draw with all this adrenaline

SEPTEMBER 16, 2007

(SIGNING BOOKS)

I WORKED HARD TODAY ON *DRAGON PUNCHER*, COMPLETING THE FINAL THREE PAGES OF THE STORY

WHILE SIMULTANEOUSLY KEEPING A VIGOROUS ARGUMENT GOING ONLINE ABOUT VIDEO GAME THEORY

CLICK CLACK CLICKY CLACKY CLACK

BASICALLY PLAYING DEVIL'S ADVOCATE... CLAIMING THAT SINCE VIDEOGAMES ARE PRIMARILY A VISUAL MEDIUM, GRAPHICS ARE OF PRIMARY IMPORTANCE AND GAMEPLAY IS SECONDARY.

CLACK CLICK

THEN WHEN ELI CAME HOME FROM PRESCHOOL:

Play Super Metroid

I'd like to but my WRiSTS are tired!

SEPTEMBER 17, 2007

REAL EVIL

Why do some strangers kill little kids?

They're Sick in the head. Look, forget I ever Said anything about it.

I think it's probably because they're trying to take over the world.

SEPTEMBER 18, 2007

CENTER FOR CARTOON STUDIES

Art blah blah comics blah blah life-

BURP

SEPTEMBER 19, 2007

ROCK

ARE you coming to the Show tonight?

Oh..yeah..if I Stay up late I'll be cranky tomorrow and RuiN my day with Eli...

Well, that's something to consider

(I DIDN'T GO)

SEPTEMBER 20, 2007

AMY'S EYELASH

Blow & make a wish

Meow?

Spandy wants it

Should I give it to her?

SEPTEMBER 21, 2007

ONLINE

(MINUTES BEFORE YESTERDAY'S STRIP:)

Come see him move

Is he done? It seems like I never really get to see him do it.

That's because you'd rather spend all your time on the computer.

What?!

No I wouldn't.

SEPTEMBER 22, 2007

SPARKLE TIME

FSSS

Our sparklers are kissing.

FSSS

Hey, Kelly. If you stare right at it, doesn't it look like a rapid series of still drawings?

FSSS

SEPTEMBER 23, 2007

ALARM KOOK

James! James!

It's NOON.

Huh?

See?

No it isn't. It's morning time.

"WELL, THEN LET'S GET UP."

SEPTEMBER 24, 2007

OCULAR DENTATA

MY EYE BIT THE BUG

BZIP

CHEWED IT UP

blink
blink
blink

AND DROOLED

SEPTEMBER 25, 2007

BLACK INK FLOWERS

I HAD MY CLASS DRAWING FLOWERS

I tell them what to do and they DO it!

BUT IT LOOKED FUN, SO I DREW ONE TOO

But how am I gonna ink it?*

Hey... do you mind if I dip in your ink?

CENTER FOR CARTOON STUDIES   SEPT. 26, 2007

* I DON'T HAVE INK IN MY BAG, I TOOK IT OUT LAST TIME I FLEW. YOU CAN'T TAKE LIQUIDS ON A PLANE SINCE IT COULD BE A BOMB INGREDIENT.

THE RIDE

Do you want to share my snacks?

PARTY CHEX

So, this beautiful young girl on the bus was really interested in talking to me.

But...

I was a little torn between my... admiration for beautiful young girls—

—and the fact that I detest talking to strangers on the bus.

SEPTEMBER 27, 2007

THROATS

AFTER SEVERAL WEEKS OF COMPLAINING I FINALLY WENT TO THE DOCTOR

On a scale of one to ten how would you rate the pain?

Zero?...

AMY CAME TOO AND HAD HER THROAT CULTURED TOO, WHILE COLBY BABYSAT

Well, that was romantic

they were all real nice to me 'cause I'm pregnant

(ELI & HALF THE KIDS IN HIS PRESCHOOL HAD STREP THROAT LAST WEEK)   SEPT 28, 2007

ONE MORE SPANDY

Hello. Oh, hi Turner.

You named your fish "Frank Spandy Allen"?

What a good girl! People are naming their little fishies after you.
KISS

SEPTEMBER 29, 2007

SPANDY'S STORY

When Eli was born, Spandy hid under the bed for three days, until I pulled her out.

Then she spent the next three years scowling at us and throwing up on the carpet, until I pretty much grew to hate her.

HISS

But now she's started sitting on my lap and loving me again, and we had the carpet replaced with hardwood floors. She's even getting used to Eli.

But the NEW baby is coming soon.

SEPTEMBER 30, 2007

LATE FOR WORK

Meow

meow — I know, Spandy.
Meow — I know
Meow — I know
meow — I know

Spandy's late for work!

She works in the basement.
Meow

OCTOBER 1, 2007

OUR DINNER WITH DECLAN

Have you ever pooped in a toilet?
No
What??
Oh. Ha ha!

Have you ever thrown up in a toilet?
Yes

Have you ever thrown up in your pants?
??

Ha ha ha ha ha ha!

OCTOBER 2, 2007

YARD POOP

Arg!

I'm sick of stepping in poop.

You're not the one pooping out here, are you?

No...

Maybe it's Declan!

OCTOBER 3, 2007

NO MORE POOP

You've got to stop drawing comics about Declan and poop!

I don't want people to associate my son with poop!

BUZZ KILL

It's cute.

I do like fluffy hair better...

This is the best I can do!

OCTOBER 4, 2007

GATHERING STICKS

DOWN THE LITTLE WOODS BEHIND OUR HOUSE

KRAK

I found something.

A dead fish? That's pretty strange.

It's HUGE

OCTOBER 5, 2007

JOB FOR SPANDY

Has it always been there?

Yes

I want to see the mouse hole!

Also Momma found mouse poop in the drawer.

OCTOBER 6, 2007

ZEETH FRUSHER

Brush your teeth.
Frush my zeeth?

Brush your teeth!
Gloff my beef?

Eli, brush your teeth.
Fluff my fleem flo floob?

BRUSH YOUR TEETH!
What did you say your name was?

OCTOBER 7, 2007

SPANDY IS DEAD

THE FISH THAT DECLAN & TURNER NAMED AFTER OUR CAT SPANDY IS DEAD. LONG LIVE SPANDY!

Spandy is like 12 years old, but she just learned how to turn the doornob to open the door to the basement

Well, then you should be able to learn to DRIVE.

OCTOBER 8, 2007

TEARS OF THE ROBOT

It's... it's not comfortable!
I can fix it

SEVERAL TRIES LATER
Waaa!
I think you're just crying 'cause you're sick

ROBOTEETH

Alright little robot...

...open your mouth and I'll brush your gears.

OCTOBER 9, 2007

X-RAY BEAR

ELI WAS HAVING TROUBLE BREATHING. THE DOCTOR SENT HIM TO THE EMERGENCY ROOM:

wheeze
WATCHING T.V.
Z

THEY GAVE HIM A TEDDY BEAR WHEN HE HAD HIS CHEST X-RAYS:

I WENT TO FIND SOME COFFEE IN THE HOSPITAL. THEY'VE GOT A RED LINE ON THE FLOOR SO YOU DON'T GET LOST

BUT I STILL GOT LOST

OCTOBER 10, 2007

PORK CHOPS ♥

Mmm! I like the fat around the edges!

Is that the part of me you like?

OCTOBER 10, 2007

FLUFFY CLOUDS

Oh my god. I want to BE there.
I've gotta draw it.

I'm gonna need FLUFFIER INK.

OCTOBER 11, 2007

After a couple years hiatus or whatever I'm finally back at the small press expo

SPX

Here I am

I'm still here

NETWORKING

AT A PARTY IN A HOTEL ROOM

I'm feeling kinda frisky, so I'd like to sing a song

BLARG ♪♫

DRUNK IN BETHESDA   OCTOBER 12, 2007

HUIZENGA 360

I might get an xbox 360.
I have a Wii

Yeah... I'd like that too. But I like the FIRST-PERSON Shooters on the 360
Well...
You know what Jesus says...

It's just as bad to think something bad as it is to DO something bad.
Even though it's "fantasy" all that killing can't be good for you.

Well... I just like the high production values of the big budget games.
And it's fun to move through space
Yeah... and to interact with stuff

SMALL PRESS EXPO, ANOTHER HOTEL ROOM PARTY   OCTOBER 13, 2007

HOME BASE

They're not here

40 MINUTES LATER:
Oh, they're so cute

Eli, I got you this little ghost

I don't want that.

OCTOBER 14, 2007

THE VIOLENT BED

"Read us a story"
"Ugh, there's no room for me"

"Eli, get off me"
KLONK

SMACK
!!!

"What's WRONG with you!"
"Hey"
BAM BAM BAM

OCTOBER 15, 2007

MEN'S ROOM

"I'm in the MEN'S ROOM at the bookstore and it said to call your NUMBER 'cause you're a slut."

"Hey, don't harass people."
"What?"
"Don't call the NUMBERS on the wall"

"Holy shit, he's going to hit me."

"No... she's my friend. I'm just warning her... you can ask her yourself"
"Is he harassing you?"

OCTOBER 16, 2007

DIM LITE

"I gave you my minicomic at SPX. Was mine one of the ones you ditched?"
"uh..."

"Well, here's another copy. I really want to know what you think."
"I'll read it on the bus."

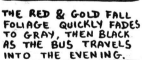

THE RED & GOLD FALL FOLIAGE QUICKLY FADES TO GRAY, THEN BLACK AS THE BUS TRAVELS INTO THE EVENING.

IT'S THE PERFECT TIME TO READ COMICS...
"Stupid light!"
"I can't Read anything"

OCTOBER 17, 2007

R4DS

"My crazy electronics from China came."

"I want to tell the WHOLE WORLD all about it, but no one would understand."

*GOOGLE IT IF YOU WANT TO KNOW.

DONKEY KONG KIDS

"Here comes another 'barrel'"

OCTOBER 18, 2004

KITTYTIME

Meow

Oh Spandy, you're so CREPUSCULAR.

CREAM puff icicle?!

I am?

No, Spandy. It means you're active in the early morning and evening

OCTOBER 19, 2007

EMPTY HEAD

James. You forgot to put kitty litter in the cat box.

I looked at it, and I knew I was doing something WRONG but I couldn't think of what it was.

OCTOBER 20, 2007

MICROMANAGEMENT

I'm speaking at UVM tomorrow and the teacher REQUIRED the students to subscribe to AMERICAN ELF.

CLICK

We've NEVER had so many people subscribe at once before. Well... there's a lot of problems.

TYPE

Some people didn't get their passwords. Other people misspelled their own email addresses!

CLICK

Maybe using the "subscription" model is STUPID. Mine is pretty much the only webcomic that does it.

OCTOBER 21, 2007

BEING AWESOME

The baby's definitely coming in just the next few weeks.

That's incredible.

I'm not sure I'm prepared.

Where have you BEEN this whole PREGNANCY?

Being awesome.

oh

OCTOBER 22, 2007

TELESCOPIC RAINDROPS

I can't see anything.

Let me try

Oh

OCTOBER 23, 2007

CATS DON'T CARE

Coming up next: The history of the space shuttle in the movies...

Ooh, Spandy! Did your hear that?

the history of the space shuttle in the movies!

KNEAD KNEAD

OCTOBER 24, 2007

NAKED LADY

AMY MADE THIS LITTLE NAKED LADY OUT OF CLAY FOR ME BACK WHEN SHE WAS IN COLLEGE

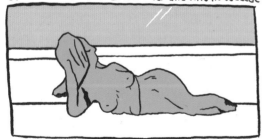

I like naked ladies!

OCTOBER 25, 2007

RIDDLES

What happens if you die before you're alive?

??? Oh! You mean like our other baby?

The first one

If you die before you're born, you never get to be a person.

WAA!

I can't believe I figured that out so fast!

OCTOBER 26, 2007

LAP SCIENTIST

Hop up on my lap Spandy, and I'll do the Rap again...

Yay!

She's got a Cat Masters in snuggling. That's S-N-U-G-G-L-ING!

She's a Lap Scientist with a PHD, She's S-P-A-N-D-y SPANDY!

Hey come back!

OCTOBER 27, 2007

PUZZLE CRIB

I've got no idea how to put the crib back together. It's like an insanely complicated puzzle

Eli don't touch any pieces! Sit on the bed till I'm done!

I can't do this! Goddamit!

ELI!

OCTOBER 28, 2007

SUPERBALL

FEELING AMY'S PREGNANT TUMMY UNDER THE BLANKET

Wow! He's bouncing around like a SUPERBALL in there!

How can you possibly sleep?

I CAN'T

OCTOBER 29, 2007

OLD COMICS

There was a six month run where Snuffy Smith's head came detached from his body.

WOW

Check this out. It's perhaps the ONLY copy of this Jimmy Swinnerton book in existance.

I think I beat Midget Eyeball in the auction

OCTOBER 30, 2007

BABY'S COSTUME

Oh! Ah! That's awesome!

Eli! Look at your brother's costume!

OCTOBER 31, 2007

OH SHIT

"IF JAMES' HEAD COULD COME DETACHED FROM HIS BODY AND FLY AROUND I'D BE IN A WORLD OF SHIT"

TYPE TYPE

JASON ♫

NOVEMBER 1, 2007

THE DARK GOD

OUR house is the DARK GOD!

The Shadow broke free from his MIND!

GASP

The breath of the DARK GOD!

NOVEMBER 2, 2007

BY YOUR COMMAND

And then I said "The breath of the DARK GOD"

But I was wearing my costume

What?

You'RE going to have to fix it

OUR HOUSE IS THE DARK GOD

NOVEMBER 3, 2007

RAKING LEAVES

WACK

I'll get the one up here

There.

No more leaves

Oh, there's one more, Eli!

Get it

NOVEMBER 4, 2007

SORRY TARGET

A PARTICLE BOARD CHANGING TABLE

It's a mistake to try to put this together NOW. I feel myself getting angry already

This thing is a peice of crap! It's broken!

Let's send it BACK

Actually, it's a big Relief!

NOVEMBER 5, 2007

UNDERGROUND

THE 3RD OF TODAY'S NUMEROUS TRIPS TO THE BASEMENT

Cat puke

There. And there. And there!

So that's what Spandy's been doing down here

Alright, I'll clean up the cat puke and you get the laundry.

ermf

NOVEMBER 6, 2007

COFFEE & ROBOT

Come ON!

I think Eli wants to play with you.

huh?

I am playing.

I've got my Robot and my cup of coffee.

NOVEMBER 7, 2007

DEFINING BEAUTIFUL

She said I am the most beautiful PREGNANT woman she's ever seen... that I look great every day

Do you thik it's true?

Sure. It all depends how you define "beautiful."

"Big and fat"

"and likes to waddle around."

NOVEMBER 8, 2007

APPLE JUICE EMERGENCY

You can have some apple juice when you're done

SOON

Look, Eli

I didn't know PREGNANT ladies could do THAT

90

NOVEMBER 9, 2007

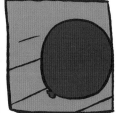

LIFE AND DEATH

ELI'S BIRTHDAY BALLOONS LASTED FOR WEEKS.

FOR MONTHS!

BUT IN THE LAST FEW DAYS...

GOODBYE BALLOONS.

I'm not dead yet!

NOVEMBER 10, 2007

DUE DATE

Andrea! Guess what's DUE ON TUESDAY?

?!

Yes, the baby. You know what else? SUPER MARIO GALAXY!

NOVEMBER 11, 2007

STING AND BURN

My lips still burn from the salt on the popcorn at the movie yesterday.

I'm sorry honey.

That's it?

NOVEMBER 11, 2007

THE WIFE'S BODY

Ow

My hip hurts
I'll rub it

Ow

Look, your pants come right down

cute bum

NOVEMBER 12, 2007

WARM PLACES

SPANDY HAS STARTED SLEEPING ON THE STOVE. SHE LIKES THE PILOT LIGHTS.

I LIKE THE WARMTH OF THE HDTV.

NOVEMBER 13, 2007

NO BABY YET

What should we name our new video game?

Mario!

Ehn. How about "Dave"?

Nooo way

My brother's name is Dave.

Yeah, let's name the game after Uncle Dave

No!

NOVEMBER 13, 2007

THE BABY IS COMING

& I'VE BEEN HAVING PANIC ATTACKS

I'm Wrestle-Wolf!

~hurk~

Cough Cough

I breathed in a little fiber from the mask!

Cough Cough

Don't panic.

Cough Cough Cough Cough!

NOVEMBER 14, 2007

HAPPILY INSANE

LAST NIGHT

TICK TOCK

The contractions are about four minutes apart.

Hey Joey, I think we're having the baby! I don't know why I called you. Cause you're my WEB GUY and you're working on my site...

THIS MORNING

How do you feel? How's the labor?

It faded away a little

NOVEMBER 15, 2007

HAPPY INSANE

She's asleep

How's the labor?

It faded away a little

I'm putting those interesting mushrooms in the scrambled eggs, Eli

I think I'll buy a new Nintendo DS today.

NOVEMBER 15, 2007

BABY ON BOARD

My vagina hurts.

I'm not joking. Just because I said "Vagina" doesn't mean I'm joking.

Ow

NOVEMBER 16, 2007

TOUCHING

Ha!

Jason says I shouldn't be playing videogames while you're so close to having the baby.

He says I should be spooning with you.

Tell Jason I don't want you to touch me.

NOVEMBER 17, 2007

MILKDRAGON

I'm the milk dragon. When you cut me, I bleed milk.

ARG!

I love being a dad

GULP GULP

NOVEMBER 18, 2007

CRAFT IS THE ENEMY

You can't make cookies without a recipe.

What? Sure I can.

But you have to measure the ingrediants.

It'll be fine

SOON

Wow! They sure PUFFED up! Cool!

Oh my god! They're terrible.

They're so bitter! Oh! Awful!

NOVEMBER 19, 2007

WELCOMING WINTER

There's frost on the roof!

That's not frost, that's SNOW!

And it's not just on the roof, it's everywhere!

NOVEMBER 20, 2007

A SPIDER ON THE WALL

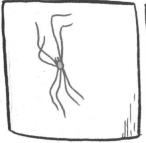

TOUCH

Happy Thanksgiving, Spider.

NOVEMBER 21, 2007

HERE HE COMES

You can see the head.

I'm a little scared but I'll take a peek

Aah!

Oh Amy! It's so amazing! Ha ha!

~ THANKSGIVING ~   NOVEMBER 22, 2007

~ INTRODUCING ~
OLIVER JONGO KOCHALKA

NOVEMBER 23, 2007

JAUNDICE

We'll put the bear in the box

And shine the special light on him.

And he'll be better soon!

NOVEMBER 24, 2007

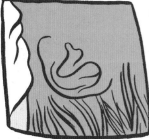

I MISS YOU SO MUCH

EVERY NIGHT THAT AMY & BABY OLIVER ARE STILL IN THE HOSPITAL, I HAVE THE SAME NIGHTMARE

RUNNING UP LITTLE PLANETS, JUMPING INTO THE STAR AND GIVING IT A SPIN

SHOOTING TO THE NEXT PLANET

AND THEN DOING IT ALL AGAIN

OVER AND OVER, ALL NIGHT LONG

NOVEMBER 25, 2007

A CONFUSING ARGUMENT

~MIDNIGHT~

I don't understand why you're talking to me in that snide, disgusted tone.

You're talking in circles! What do you want me to say?

Just say "Yes, I hate you" or "No, I don't"

No, I don't.

NOVEMBER 26, 2007

LITTLE MAN

You are SUCH a strange little man!

NOVEMBER 27, 2007

BROTHERS

Ah Ah

He said his first word! "Ah"

Now that I have a brother I love him even more than I love my parents!

NOVEMBER 28, 2007

~ROOT HOG OR DIE!!~
SNURFER

Snorf

Sorry Sweetie. There's no nipple in my ear.

Snerf

BWAA

NOVEMBER 29, 2007

☆ OUCHIES ★

I had a dream that I was rubbing your yin-yang.

But I woke up quick because I thought I was really doing it & I know I'm not supposed to!

Noooo! Don't really do it.

NOVEMBER 30, 2007

LITTLE PAINS OF BEING

Ever since I started cooking dinner, my fingertips hurt.

Because I always burn them!

...and your hip hurts from walking and your wrist hurts from playing videogames

Well, yeah

LIFE HURTS!

Oh, I know.

DECEMBER 1, 2007

TRUE CONFESSIONS

OLIVER WAS BORN WITH ONE TINY WHITE PIMPLE.

maybe I can—

Good! It finally came off

Oh, but Amy will be mad that I did that.

LATER:

Hmm, she hasn't noticed. I guess I'll just confess

DECEMBER 2, 2007

WINTER HOT

WET WITH SNOW AND HOT FROM PLAYING

Eli, your body is STEAMING!

I can't see it

DECEMBER 3, 2007

FIRST FURY

GRRR

ATTACK!

PCHOW

So easily defeated! But... one day... OLIVER will have HIS REVENGE!

DECEMBER 4, 2007

LIVING MUSIC

My footsteps sound like music, don't they?

And my snow pants

TAP TAP

SHZING

It's like some kinda tappy drum and a whistle.

ZING   SHZING   TAP TAP TAP

DECEMBER 5, 2007

DIGITAL FREAK

SO... WE FINALLY LAUNCHED THE NEWLY REDESIGNED VERSION OF AMERICANELF.COM AND THEN THE SERVER CRASHED.

Amy, my website is STILL down!

Just stop checking it. Do something else.

But I'm freaking out!

And I'm going to keep on freaking out until it's fixed

DECEMBER 6, 2007

CHILDREN'S MUSIC

"I hear beautiful music"

PLUNK PLUNK

"This guitar is evil"

"And this song is called "kill all the people""

DECEMBER 7, 2007

AWESOME POWER

"Oliver has too much SQUIGGLE POWER!"

"Too much wiggle flour?"

"We must've used too much wiggle flour when we baked him"

DECEMBER 8, 2007

TRUE TOE STORY

ON THE DAY OLIVER WAS BORN I WORE MY SHOES ALL DAY

"Maybe I should take my shoes off"

"My water's about to break"

"I'll keep them on!!"

I NEVER WEAR SHOES ALL DAY. THE SWEAT MADE THE SKIN BETWEEN TWO OF MY TOES JUST SORTA ROT OFF. BUT NOW, TWO WEEKS LATER...

"Almost all better"

DECEMBER 8, 2007

SPANDY HAS SOMETHING TO SAY

"Meow! Meow!"

"Meow Meow! Meow! Meow!"

"Meow!" "Meow" "Meow" "Meow"

"Does it still count as "Postpartum psychosis" if you don't want to harm your baby but you want to harm your cat?"

DECEMBER 9, 2007

I ALWAYS YELL

There! It's up!

And I didn't even yell at anyone this year! *

Yay!

* AMY GOT A NEW TREE STAND. IT'S EASIER THAN OUR OLD ONE.

DECEMBER 10, 2007

PART TWO

I'm so glad I didn't yell at anyone while setting up the tree this year

Eli!

!?

You're standing on the LIGHTS!

Oh no! I did yell this year.

DECEMBER 11, 2007

SHINING LOVE

Look, Oliver. Your Daddy is drawing

Oh, he loves the windows and the lightbulb more than Daddy.

They're just SO bright!

DECEMBER 12, 2007

snuf snuf hooink

Shnuf snuf quink glorp

Shlorp :snuf: hoink hoink glarp :Shnorf: GROOOINK

THE SOUNDS OF BREASTFEEDING

DECEMBER 13, 2007

UP THE HILL

ARRG!

I'm filling in your footsteps so you don't have to worry about them.

But who's going to fill in YOUR footprints?

DECEMBER 14, 2007

PHOTOCOPY LOVE

I wish I had a photo' of myself.

A photocopy of yourself?

Yeah

Then one could love mommy and one could love you.

But the Real one would love mommy.

What?

Hey!

DECEMBER 15, 2007

CARDBOARD

We can use this cardboard as a sled.

No thanks

DECEMBER 16, 2007

LOGIC & MAGIC

I want a teleporter for Christmas

But teleporters aren't real

Yeah they are

Teleporters are things... and things are Real.

Is Oliver me?

DECEMBER 17, 2007

THE REFLECTION
OF MY DRAWING
LAMP IN THE
INK IN THE
BOTTLE CAP

12/17/2007

I AM INSANE

CONFRONTING A GUY GOING INTO THE
NEIGHBOR'S APARTMENT

Hey, are you going in there to buy DRUGS?

What?! No.

Cause if you are, I wish you wouldn't.

Why don't you go buy drugs in your own neighborhood

You're not the owner of this street! Who asked you?!

SOON We're gonna smash your windows. We're gonna smash your car!

You're gonna need a new fuckin' house!

DECEMBER 18, 2007

AWAITING MY FATE

MY HEAD IS KILLING ME

I'M STRESSED OUT, JUMPING AT EVERY SOUND

BUT ALSO KINDA PROUD OF MYSELF

Yeah it was a stupid thing to do...

...but, that's how I Roll

DECEMBER 19, 2007

IT'S A MAGICAL WORLD

Hey BRUCE! I'm still alive!!

DECEMBER 20, 2007

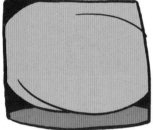

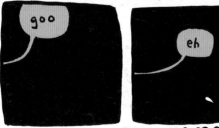

WEIRD SWEATERS

I guess it's a fine sweater

It feels weird though.

My fingers feel all waxy or something now.

Aah! That's weird!

DECEMBER 25, 2007

THE FROZEN MEADOW

SWISH
FWAK

SHUK

DECEMBER 26, 2007

BLUE SWEATPANTS

Sweatpants!

I set out real pants for him and you let him switch!

All the kids his age wear sweatpants

Come on James, let's play.

I'm too mad now

I'm so mean

DECEMBER 27, 2007

SPIRALS

I'VE BEEN IN A DOWNWARD SPIRAL

MY BEHAVIOR IS ERATIC & OFTEN MEAN

I'M AN ATHIEST, BUT

Should I tell her that I've been praying?

DECEMBER 28, 2007

WHAT'S FOR DINNER

Do you think your mother will *Really* have dinner ready for us?

No

Maybe she'll have some old chicken bones she brought home from church.

We can suck the marrow from those.

DECEMBER 28, 2007

BLACK DOOM

Noooo

The ink leaked all over my new Nintendo DS.

And grandma's rug

I CAREFULLY FIXED CHARLOTTE'S RUG BY CLIPPING THE DRIED INK AWAY WITH TOENAIL SCISSORS, BUT

ink in my DS...

I'm so stupid my brain can't even think

N. SPRINGFIELD, VT

DECEMBER 29, 2007

LIFETIME

Who is that?

Oliver Jonco Kochalka.

Gluck

Jonco?! That's me!

They called me Jonco when I was a little boy

SPRINGFIELD, VT

DECEMBER 30, 2007

GOODBYE 2007

I AM AN ATHEIST WITH A DEEP, PERSONAL RELATIONSHIP WITH GOD

I AM CERTAIN THERE'S NO GOD EVEN THOUGH I DEEPLY FEEL THE PRESENCE OF THE DIVINE ALL AROUND ME. I SENSE THE MAGIC AND POWER IN EVERYTHING.

OFTEN, I BARELY FEEL LIKE I EVEN HAVE "FREE WILL". SO MUCH OF WHAT I THINK AND FEEL SEEMS CHEMICAL AND BEYOND MY CONTROL...

SO... LET IT GO AND JUST LISTEN TO THE DIVINE.

Listen! Listen to the sound the sled is making!

SSSZZEEEEN

DECEMBER 31, 2007

KOCHALKA FAMILY PHOTOS
2006 - 2007